AMERICAN HORTICULTURAL SOCIETY
PRACTICAL GUIDES

ANNUALS &
BIENNIALS

AMERICAN HORTICULTURAL SOCIETY
PRACTICAL GUIDES

ANNUALS & BIENNIALS

CHRISTOPHER GREY-WILSON

DORLING KINDERSLEY PUBLISHING, INC.
www.dk.com

HE JB GP
PR PH GB DP [DK] EG VWM HB WR

DORLING KINDERSLEY PUBLISHING, INC.
www.dk.com

Project Editor Annelise Evans
Art Editor Ursula Dawson

Senior Editor Gillian Roberts
Series Art Editor Stephen Josland
US Editor Ray Rogers

Senior Managing Editor Mary-Clare Jerram
Managing Art Editor Lee Griffiths

DTP Designer Louise Paddick

Production Controller Mandy Inness

First American edition, 2000
2 4 6 8 10 9 7 5 3 1

Published in the United States by
Dorling Kindersley Publishing, Inc., 95 Madison Avenue, New York, NY 10016

Dorling Kindersley Publishing, Inc. offers special discounts for bulk purchases for sales
promotions or premiums. Specific, large-quantity needs can be met with special editions,
including personalized covers, excerpts of existing guides, and corporate imprints.
For more information, contact Special Markets Department, Dorling Kindersley
Publishing, Inc., 95 Madison Avenue, New York, NY 10016 Fax: 800-600-9098.

Library of Congress Cataloging-in-Publication Data

Grey-Wilson, Christopher.
    Annuals and biennials / [Christopher Grey-Wilson]. -- 1st American
ed.
        p. cm. -- (AHS practical guides)
        ISBN 0-7894-5066-6 (alk. paper)
        1. Annuals (Plants)   2. Biennials (Plants)   I. Title   II. Series.
    SB422.G74 2000
    635.9'312--dc21   99-38067
                                                  CIP
Reproduced by Colourscan, Singapore
Printed and bound by Star Standard Industries, Singapore

CONTENTS

USING ANNUALS AND BIENNIALS

WHAT ARE ANNUALS AND BIENNIALS?

AN ANNUAL PLANT, IN BOTANICAL TERMS, is one that completes its life cycle – from the germinating seed to a mature flowering plant, followed by fruit-set and seed production – within a single growing season, often in just a few months. Annuals are therefore fast-growing plants, often producing a mass of colorful flowers. Biennials take two growing seasons to fulfill their life cycles, germinating in the first year then flowering, fruiting, and dying in the second.

HARDINESS TO COLD

Many annuals and biennials are quite hardy and withstand freezing conditions, surviving winter as seeds that come up the following spring (annuals) or as plants (biennials). These can usually be sown directly in the garden, in autumn or spring, or put in the garden as transplants. Some annuals and biennials tolerate some cold but not frost. They must be sown under cover in late winter or early spring for planting out after the last frost. Many popular annuals, such as petunias and nicotiana, will not stand any frost and suffer in temperatures below 41°F (5°C). These very tender annuals must be planted out once all risk of frost has passed and the soil has warmed up.

◄ FAST ANNUAL
Many fast-growing annuals, such as this nasturtium, Tropaeolum *Alaska Series, produce a mass of colorful flowers within a few weeks from seed.*

◄ACCENTUATE THE VERTICAL *Mulleins and red orache bring quick height to a border.*

▲ SPIKY BIENNIAL
*Typical biennials, including
the showy common foxglove*
(Digitalis purpurea), *form
a rosette of leaves in the first
year and send up flowering
stems in the second.*

► FIERY ANNUAL
A drift of Zinnia haageana
*'Persian Carpet' produces
a blaze of color throughout
the summer months.*

Most annuals are easy to grow in the garden, whether or not they need to be started off indoors. They quickly form a mass of color, primarily in summer and early autumn, although some flower in spring. By sowing seed of many of them in batches, the display can be extended over many weeks. Annuals come in a huge range of colors, sizes, and textures and can be used for many different styles of planting.

Gardeners value annuals for their bright display of flowers, suited to modern small yards, for formal bedding designs, and for container planting, but some annuals also make excellent cut flowers, foliage plants, subjects for drying, or for enticing insects and other wildlife into the garden.

The range of options can be extended with biennials such as sweet William and some of the mulleins (*Verbascum*), whether grown in a separate area and then planted out, or sown direct to flower the next year.

PERENNIALS GROWN AS ANNUALS

A number of short-lived garden perennials (plants that live for more than two years) are grown from seed as annuals to flower in their first year. These include familiar

TRADITIONAL FAVORITES

ANNUALS	BIENNIALS	PERENNIALS GROWN
Centaurea cyanus	*Campanula medium*	AS ANNUALS
Helianthus annuus	*Dianthus barbatus*	*Antirrhinum majus*
Portulaca grandiflora	*Digitalis purpurea*	*Begonia semperflorens*
Zinnia elegans	*Lunaria annua*	*Impatiens walleriana*

plants such as the small bedding dahlias, impatiens, including the New Guinea hybrids, and many types of geranium (*Pelargonium*). Quite a few plants sold for annual bedding are in fact perennials. Although they are often discarded at the end of the season in cold climates, many can be overwintered under cover as plants grown from rooted cuttings.

GROWING PLANTS TOGETHER

Few gardens are devoted solely to annuals and biennials – these are just one element in a varied planting that may include trees, shrubs, perennials, and bulbs. Annuals are often grown on their own in a border for maximum impact, but they can combine well with other plants – in containers, for instance, or to fill gaps in herbaceous beds.

Later in this book, you will find some suggested plantings for annuals and biennials in the garden. Alternatives can be found in Choice Annuals and Biennials (*see pp.60–77*), and good nurseries and garden centers should also offer an excellent selection of suitable plants and seeds.

▲ EXUBERANT ANNUAL BORDER
This attractive border consists of vivid drifts of coreopsis, dahlias, salpiglossis, and zinnias.

◄ A MIXED BORDER
An impression of a bank of wildflowers has been created here by mixing together some snapdragons, cornflowers, and pansies with an informal planting of perennials.

PLANTING IDEAS

THERE IS ROOM FOR ANNUALS AND BIENNIALS in even the smallest garden. Baskets, floral pillars, and windowboxes can be crammed with vibrant flowers and foliage to excite the eye for many months of the year. More plants can be worked into the herbaceous border or scattered among shrubs to liven up permanent plantings with seasonal color. A container brimming with petunias or pansies can be a stunning focal point on a patio or balcony.

MIXING AND MATCHING PLANTS

If you have a large enough garden to devote an entire bed to a summer display, then an annual border can be the high point of the year. However, combining annuals and biennials with other planting opens up a world of possible combinations of color, form, and texture. For new beds, borders, or gardens, annuals and biennials, particularly bedding plants, are extremely useful for furnishing almost instant color and interest while permanent members of the planting display establish.

The structure of existing borders is usually provided by small trees and shrubs as well as herbaceous perennials. The look of the borders can be transformed from year to year by using annuals and biennials to note the changes of the seasons. Most annuals are fairly shallow-rooted and thrive among deep-rooted perennials. Annuals grow best in an open, sunny situation and dislike being overshadowed by trees and shrubs, so in smaller gardens, some thinning of existing trees and shrubs may be needed to allow the annuals to perform at their best.

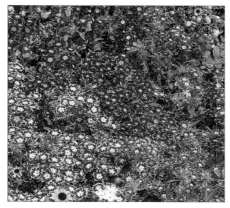

▲ PAINTING WITH PLANTS
The traditional way to grow annuals is to sow or plant them in drifts to paint a seasonal bed or border with blocks of color, as with this pretty Phlox drummondii *'Sternenzauber'.*

► ORNAMENTAL KITCHEN GARDEN
Annual calendulas and borage are perfect in an informal vegetable garden; as well as being colorful foils to these decorative cabbages, the flowers are edible.

However, a few annuals – especially impatiens – prefer dappled shade and are ideal for brightening up more enclosed spots.

For instant height, use annuals and biennials with tall flower spikes, such as foxgloves, or even sunflowers. Annual climbers such as Canary creeper or morning glories can be encouraged to scramble over and through shrubs or up a tepee of stakes to create a colorful focal point.

Felicitous plant associations can happen by chance if annuals and biennials are left to seed about the garden – simply weed out any plants that pop up in inappropriate

Annuals and biennials add temporary structure to a border

places – but it is worth planning to assure a successful display. Try mixing forget-me-nots, honesty, poached-egg plants, pansies, and wallflowers with spring-flowering bulbs, such as daffodils, hyacinths, and tulips, or, in summer, grow corn cockles, larkspurs, love-in-a-mist, and poppies with bulbs such as alliums, gladioli, and irises.

▲ DYNAMIC DUO
Brilliant yellow corn marigolds and hot red poppies, both quick-growing annuals, make a dramatic summer combination.

▼ GOOD ENOUGH TO EAT
Annual and perennial edible herbs (here nasturtiums, pansies, and calendulas, with perennial purple sage and variegated mint) are planted together in a bank of color to form an appetizing alliance.

ANNUAL SEED MIXTURES

MOST ANNUALS ARE IDEAL for sowing directly in the garden, especially when a naturalistic effect is required, since the seeds of many different plants can be mixed and sown together. All you need to do is to prepare the soil, sow the seed mixture at the appropriate time, and then stand back and wait for the results. The consequent medley of pretty flowers of varying hues, forms, and heights will suggest the casual harmony of nature.

NATURAL BEAUTY

Many annuals, especially the species, have a simplicity of flower and form that lends itself to naturalistic designs in a garden. Whereas blended seed mixtures produce displays that look a little out of place in a formal setting, they are perfect for borders in an informal or a cottage-garden style. Naturalistic mixes also attract insects and birds into the garden.

A patch of uncultivated or recently tilled soil in the garden, preferably one that has not been enriched with fertilizers, presents an opportunity to create a charming swath of annuals that recalls wildflower meadows of times past. If perennials and woody plants are kept out and the wildflowers allowed to go to seed, some seed mixes will reappear for many years.

Seed dealers offer a wide range of attractive seed mixtures of annuals: for cool or hot color schemes, for cutting, to grow for scent, wildflower mixtures, and quick-growing assortments for children to try.

Change the look of your garden by sowing a new seed mixture each year

Yet half the fun is to make up your own mixture. For a successful blend, choose seeds of plants that will look good with one another and are about the same height, although some differences in height can result in a pleasingly tiered effect. Annuals with small flowers, such as daisies, or

BLOWSY BORDER
This planting relies on blues and purples, studded with a few bright colors, to create a pretty drift of flowers that will also attract pollinating insects.

◄MEADOW MIX
*Annual species, such
as blue cornflowers,
white daisies, scarlet
poppies, and yellow
corn marigolds, create
a brilliantly colored
summer composition.*

▼COTTAGE GARDEN
*Annuals are the
mainstay of old-style
cottage gardening, in
which beds spill over
with a colorful
patchwork of flowers.*

simple blooms such as cornflowers, will
look more natural than showy garden
cultivars, such as double zinnias. Add seeds
of willowy annual grasses for an airy effect.
You may want to choose flowers that
mature at about the same time to enjoy the
full impact of the display.

SOWING SEED MIXTURES

When preparing your own mixture, be sure
to mix the seeds thoroughly; adding fine
sand to the mix will help you sow the seeds
thinly and evenly. Overly thick sowings will
require a good deal of thinning at the
seedling stage to ensure a good display. It
is also important to choose the right seed
mixture for your soil; otherwise, the results
are likely to be disappointing. Specialty
wildflower firms sell annual mixtures, or
mixtures of annuals and perennials, for
many different soil types.

In many areas, annuals can be sown
directly once the soil is warm enough, but
in cold climates, some plants may need to
be raised under cover and planted out
randomly to produce the same effect as
sowing a mixture.

PLANTS FOR COLOR

THINK OF A COLOR, and you are almost bound to find an annual or biennial in that hue. Use the color wheel (*right*) to help you explore the way in which colors relate to each other and the effects of different color combinations in the garden. You can learn a lot about use of color by visiting other gardens and noting the most pleasing color associations.

COLOR WHEEL

THE COLOR WHEEL

Three primary colors – blue, yellow, and red – form the basis of the color wheel. These blend together to produce secondary colors – purple, green, and orange – between them; where the segments meet are many gradations of shade and hue. Colors farthest apart on the wheel produce the strongest contrasts, such as purple and yellow or blue and orange. Using plants with hues from opposing segments of the color wheel can produce a dazzling, and sometimes shocking, effect that may be lively and eye-catching from a distance. Some plants produce their own stark contrasts: the brilliant red flowers of the corn poppy contrast vividly with its own bright green foliage; some pansies strikingly combine hot yellows and deep purples in their blooms. In contrast, neighboring

BASIC COLORS
Plants of a single color may be used in a monochromatic planting, with shades of the same hue, or with other colors. Use white flowers as cooling highlights.

MOLUCCELLA LAEVIS

ZINNIA ELEGANS
'DREAMLAND SCARLET'

ERYSIMUM CHEIRI
'FIRE KING'

ESCHSCHOLZIA CALIFORNICA
'YELLOW CAP'

NEMESIA VERSICOLOR
'BLUE BIRD'

colors, such as blue and green, or pink and purple, produce softer, more harmonious effects. For example, the pink flowers of a cornflower find a subtle foil in its silky-haired, gray-green leaves, while the delicate blue flowers of love-in-a-mist are softened further by its finely dissected green foliage.

If space is limited, sow a single species with mixed flower colors

When planning color combinations, do not forget the importance of foliage: gray or silver foliage, such as that of *Senecio cineraria*, can subtly complement blue and white flowers; coleus (*Solenostemon*) has leaves in vivid golds, reds, and purples.

PLANNING COLOR SCHEMES

Experimenting with color when using annuals and biennials in the garden can be fun but also daunting. It helps to work out the plant combinations roughly on paper before sowing or planting. Go for color schemes that really appeal to you.

Your choice will also depend to some extent on the effect that you are trying to create. Interestingly, bold, hot colors such as orange and gold make plants much more prominent, whereas cool colors like pink, white, and blue have a more impressionistic effect and create an illusion of distance.

The impact of the planting will also be influenced by other features in the garden, especially the colors of surrounding trees and shrubs. The varying heights of the plants and their flowering periods will play a key role in the effectiveness of the design.

IPOMOEA PURPUREA 'GRANDPA OTT'

CLEOME HASSLERIANA 'HELEN CAMPBELL'

VIOLA 'ROMEO AND JULIET'
Some cultivars have flowers of harmonious mixed colors.

USING HOT COLORS

H OT, VIBRANT COLORS WORK wonderfully well in warmer regions, but vivid reds, yellows, and oranges, liberally used, can produce an impression of warmth even during cool summers in more cooler climates. Among annuals and biennials, the hotter colors are almost exclusively restricted to summer- and autumn-flowering plants; they perfectly complement the autumnal coloration of surrounding trees and shrubs with their reds, oranges, and bronzes.

SEASONAL BRILLIANCE

In early summer, the brilliant scarlet annual poppies display their tissue-paper blooms, and the clear yellows and golds of the California poppies are at their best. As the summer wears on, more and more brightly hued annuals appear, from the various sorts of marigold (*Tagetes*) and zinnia to the handsome rudbeckias in colors from lemon yellow to gold and rusty red, which prolong the season well into autumn.

From midsummer onward, a succession of salvias in reds, purples, and bright pinks, and similarly colored dahlias and dianthus, grace the garden. This vivid cornucopia of color is brought to a close only by the first frosts of autumn.

Subtle is not the word to describe the exuberant reds, oranges, and yellows of summer annuals and biennials. You can use them to create hot spots in beds and borders that draw the eye along the garden.

GLOWING FOLIAGE
There is no need for dazzling flowers when the foliage is brightly hued, as with this bank of coleus, Solenostemon *Wizard Series. The leaves echo the yellow of the ivy,* Hedera helix *'Buttercup', behind. Each plant of coleus may display a slightly different combination of colors or patterns. Ideal for summer bedding, coleus also make splendid container plants.*

▲ RED-HOT PINKS
Dianthus *Telstar Series comes
in a mixture of red and pink
shades; the lighter tones
accentuate the fiery scarlet,
providing a spectacular show.*

◄ EVERLASTING COLOR
The vividly clashing colors of
Bracteantha bracteata *may be
preserved by drying them to
brighten winter days.*

Deep yellow and orange cosmos set among
blood red celosia and multicolored lantanas
form a bold combination that certainly
cannot be overlooked. The choice of warm-
colored annuals and biennials is almost
endless, but it can be a mistake to overplay
the hot colors. They may be simply too
busy and hectic. Other, more subtle
contrasts may often prove far more
effective. For instance, bright orange and
red shades can look splendid against the
purple foliage of *Atriplex* or red-leaved
Amaranthus, while deep purple salvias may
be greatly enhanced by the yellow-green
foliage of *Smyrnium*.

Contrasting flower form and shape may
add interest, especially when upright spikes
of plants such as verbascums are set against
rounded flowerheads of pompon dahlias or
large-flowered marigolds.

HOT-COLORED ANNUALS

RED
Celosia argentea
Pelargonium
Salvia splendens

ORANGE
Cosmos sulphureus
Lantana camara
Tithonia rotundifolia

YELLOW
Rudbeckia hirta
Tagetes
Zinnia

MAGENTA
Petunia
Portulaca grandiflora
Verbena

USING COOL COLORS

M OST GARDENS NEED COOL BORDERS to give an airy feeling of freshness and space. However, a mass planting of annuals and biennials in cool colors, especially blue, white, and pale pink, may prove to be bland and uninspiring unless enhanced with pale and matte greens, subtle creams, and soft yellows. Occasionally, stronger, contrasting colors can be introduced as highlights or even deliberate clashes or disturbances in the overall harmony of the border.

PALE AND INTERESTING

Planting designs in cool colors become very prominent and almost luminous in the dusk of evening and at night, when hot colors fade into the gloom. They also recede into the distance and create an impression of space in the garden.

When planning a cool combination, try not to mix too many blues and pale pinks: moderation in the choice of plants is the key to success, because too many different shades will look fussy rather than soothing.

COOL COMBINATIONS

Try blending the pure blue blooms and feathery green foliage of love-in-a-mist (*Nigella damascena*) with the spikes of pink larkspur (*Consolida ajacis*), the delicate pastel shades of the tissue-thin petals of *Papaver rhoeas* 'Mother of Pearl', and the white mistiness of *Gypsophila elegans*. If more greens are required, think about adding some of the annual grasses, such as the fountain grass (*Pennisetum setaceum*). The whole effect of the planting can be light, restful, and meadowlike.

PURE WHITE BOUNDARIES
The white flowers of petunias and feverfew (Tanacetum parthenium) *against green foliage make a soft, yet elegant, edge to a pathway.*

COOL-COLORED ANNUALS

CREAMS AND WHITES	Callistephus chinensis	Iberis umbellata
Cosmos bipinatus	Nemophila menziesii	
Digitalis purpurea f. albiflora	Nigella damascena	PINKS
Ipomoea tricolor		Begonia semperflorens
Lavatera trimestris	LILACS, MAUVES, AND VIOLETS	Catharanthus roseus
Mirabilis jalapa		Cleome hassleriana
	Brachyscome iberidifolia	Impatiens walleriana
BLUES	Browallia speciosa	Nicotiana alata
Ageratum houstonianum	Heliotropium arborescens	Zinnia

◄STAR PLANT
Nemophila maculata
*is a pretty little
annual that makes an
excellent subject for
the edge of a cool
border. It is stunning
with blue lobelias or
Swan River daisies*
(Brachyscome).

▼A COOL BORDER
Lobelias, Nemesia
*'Fragrant Cloud', and
pansies create a study
in blue and white,
contrasted with the
soft gray foliage of*
Helichrysum petiolare
'Variegatum'.

For a very dramatic display, try planting a
border composed only of blue-flowered
annuals and biennials. An all-white border
can seem almost wintry, even at the height
of summer. The occasional introduction of
pleasing foliage plants, whether annual,
biennial, or short-lived perennials, (for
instance, silver-leaved *Senecio cineraria*

Deep green or purple foliage makes a dramatic contrast to pale blooms

or the fresh green of the burning bush
(*Bassia scoparia* f. *trichophylla*) can
heighten the sense of quiet beauty. The
spiky biennial Miss Willmott's ghost
(*Eryngium giganteum*) and the perennial
lamb's ears (*Stachys byzantina*), with silver-
gray, furry foliage, also offer contrasts in
leaf color and texture to highlight and
complement the main color scheme.
　Above all, never be afraid to experiment.
Annuals and biennials are short-lived
seasonal plants, so if you do not get it quite
right one year, there is always the next.

ANNUALS AND BIENNIALS FOR DRYING

S PRING AND SUMMER ARE THE SEASONS in which annuals and biennials hold the stage, but long after the summer flowers have withered away in the garden, dried arrangements indoors can prolong the display and remind you of the glories of the past summer. Many annuals and some biennials lend themselves to drying. Carefully dried flowers retain their color well and, if kept in a dry atmosphere, will last for at least twelve months until the next harvest is ready.

PRESERVING PERFECTION

The vivid colors of fresh annual and biennial flowers can become quite muted in the drying process, but the subtle, earthy tones of naturally dried flowers are very pleasing. In contrast, commercially dried flowers are often dyed in brash and unnatural hues. The form and texture of dried flowers is as important as the colors. Look for strong shapes, such as the elegant cups of bells of Ireland (*Moluccella laevis*) or the spiky bracts and leaves of sea holly (*Eryngium*), and interesting textures, such

as the papery heads of strawflowers (*Bracteantha bracteata*). Seedheads can look as handsome as flowers when dried, whether displayed in arrangements on their own or mixed with dried flowers.

To avoid spoiling displays in the flower garden, try setting aside a small plot (part of the vegetable garden, for instance) to grow annuals and biennials specifically for drying. Here, they can be sown and grown in neat rows until they are ready to be cut; sow grasses more thickly than usual so that their slender stems support each other.

LONG-LASTING COLOR
Statice (Limonium sinuatum) *is a long-flowering annual, widely used as a dried flower and available in a variety of colors. Cut sprays can be hung upside down in bunches to dry and have a decorative charm all their own.*

PEPPER SHAKERS
The fat seed capsules of the opium poppy (Papaver somniferum) are among the most decorative of all annuals. Dried pods look very dramatic in arrangements and in winter wreaths and garlands.

DRYING FLOWERS AND FRUITS

Take care to select flowers for drying that are half open; most fully mature flowers will not dry well. Plants with large, delicate flowers, such as clarkias or poppies, are not suitable for drying. Cut single flowers or sprays with long stems, and strip off large leaves and damaged or overblown flowers.

Tie the stems in small bunches with soft string or raffia, then hang them upside down to dry in an airy, warm, dry place, out of direct sun. Once thoroughly dried, cut the bunches down and make them into

---

Use dried flowers and fruits in swags, wreaths, and potpourris

---

arrangements. Take care when handling dried flowers because they are quite fragile.

The method for drying and preserving fruits is the same as for flowers. The best time to gather fruits and seed capsules for drying is when they are fully mature and are just starting to dry out naturally. If left too long in the garden, they will often become discolored or fall apart.

Annual grasses are also excellent for drying. The timing is critical: cut too early and the stems will be too soft and thin to support the heads, but if cut too late the spikelets will begin to fall apart at the slightest touch. Generally, the best time to cut grasses for drying is when the lower spikelets in the heads come into flower (generally signified by the appearance of the yellow or cream stamens).

GOOD PLANTS FOR DRYING

Bracteantha bracteata	*Moluccella laevis*
Briza maxima	*Onopordum acanthium*
Consolida ajacis	*Psylliostachys suworowii*
Eryngium giganteum	
Gomphrena globosa	*Trachelium caeruleum*
Limonium sinuatum	*Xeranthemum annuum*

LUNARIA ANNUA

PROLONGING THE SEASON

AFTER THE RICH DISPLAYS OF BLOOM have faded, many flowering annuals also produce very decorative seedheads, changing the focus of the display from lush color to starker forms, textures, and subtle harvest tones well into the autumn and winter. Annual grasses echo the mood, their plumes becoming more feathery and bleached as they go to seed. A few annuals and biennials add spots of color with glossy fruits in festive scarlet.

FRUITFUL HARVEST

Some annuals, such as marigolds (*Tagetes*), impatiens, zinnias, dahlias, and petunias, are grown only for their flowers, so deadheading is important in prolonging the display. However, if you avoid the temptation to clear away other annuals at the end of summer, you can enjoy annuals with ornamental fruits and the fascinating variety of those with attractive seedheads.

Bring zest to the summer border with the chili pepper (*Capsicum annuum*) – its many cultivars have tapering fruits in fiery

reds, purples, and yellows. You could continue the theme indoors with the bright winter cherry (*Solanum pseudocapsicum*).

The scope for using seedheads is even greater. Annual honesty (*Lunaria annua*) has tissue-thin, papery disks with a silvery sheen; those of love-in-a-mist (*Nigella damascena*) look like little horned balloons, while those of poppies (*Papaver*) resemble pepper shakers. California poppies (*Eschscholzia*) produce long, slender, sickle-shaped pods. The imposing biennial *Onopordum acanthium* has long-lasting,

▲ VERSATILE SUNFLOWER
*This gaudy annual daisy (here
Helianthus 'Pastiche') is a star
performer in the garden, is
excellent for cutting or for
drying as a winter decoration,
and has edible seeds.*

▶ DECORATIVE HERB
*Dill is an aromatic annual
widely used as a culinary
herb. The flat clusters of seeds
are very ornamental and can
be dried for winter use.*

▲ QUAKING GRASS
This fast-growing annual grass is named after its locket-shaped seedheads, which rattle in the slightest breeze.

◄ AGING GRACEFULLY
Grasses such as foxtail barley fluff out and fade to beige as they go to seed and add lightness to plants like these perennial Gaura lindheimeri.

thistlelike seedheads. The biggest and boldest of them all is the sunflower, with flat disks of hundreds of symmetrically arranged seeds, a study in geometry.

Besides their ornamental value, the fruits and seedheads are the source of seed that may be gathered for the following year's display (*see pp.56–57*) or in some cases for culinary use, or left on the plant over the winter to provide food for wild birds.

GRACIOUS GRASSES

The sleek, silky, or distinctly fuzzy flower clusters or spikelets of annual grasses improve with age, becoming fluffier and more delicately colored as they go to seed. They often persist for months into winter. Grasses tone down excesses of hot summer borders and can create a marvelously impressionistic look when used with pastel flowers. Later, rimed with frost, they take on an ethereal magic all their own.

RECOMMENDED

DECORATIVE FRUITS
Capsicum annuum; Solanum pseudocapsicum

DECORATIVE SEEDPODS
*Argemone; Atriplex hortensis
Cardiospermum halicacabum
Consolida ajacis; Dipsacus fullonum
Eccremocarpus scaber
Glaucium corniculatum; Lablab purpureus
Nigella damascena; Papaver somniferum
Ricinus communis; Scabiosa stellata*

EDIBLE SEEDS
*Anethum graveolens; Coriandrum sativum
Foeniculum vulgare; Helianthus annuus
Zea mays*

GRASSES
*Briza maxima; Hordeum jubatum
Lagurus ovatus; Pennisetum setaceum
Setaria italica*

ANNUAL CLIMBING PLANTS

SOME OF THE MOST BEAUTIFUL AND POPULAR of the flowering annuals are climbers. Most are fast-growing and excellent for punctuating a border with a pillar of bloom, dressing an arch or pergola, disguising an unsightly structure, or creating an exuberant wall of summer color. Combined with bushy annuals, they extend the surge of flowers upward and, if allowed to scramble among herbaceous perennials and shrubs, they add a pleasing touch of informality.

CROWNING GLORIES

The queen of annual climbing plants is arguably the sweet pea (*Lathyrus odoratus*), prized for its beautiful, sweetly perfumed flowers in many attractive hues. It dislikes hot, dry areas, growing to perfection in cooler regions. Few annual climbers make finer cut flowers. Where sweet peas fail, other annual climbers will thrive, producing a mass of lovely blooms and fresh green foliage in a short space of time to add to the sense of abundance in the spring and summer garden. Morning

Liven up the evergreen of ivy with bright blooms of annual climbers

glories (*Ipomoea*) are especially impressive, being rampant growers that open vividly colored trumpets over a long season.

Most annual climbers can also be grown in large containers to form a feature for courtyards or patios or allowed to creep

SWEET PEAS
Sweet peas may be trained up a 8ft (2.5m) tepee of stakes or on netting or a trellis.

Tepee made of 8–10 stakes inserted in a circle and tied together at top

PRACTICAL TIPS

• Most annual climbers dislike being transplanted, so sow several seeds to a small pot, thin out to one seedling, and grow on.
• Alternatively, when the air and soil are warm enough, sow seed directly.
• Place supports in position in the garden before direct sowing or planting to avoid damaging young plants, especially the roots.
• Allow plenty of space and headroom – annual climbers can be very vigorous. Also, make sure the supports are strong enough to withstand the weight of the plants and the force of strong winds from storms.
• Pinch out growing tips of young plants to encourage bushy growth.
• Deadhead the plants regularly to prolong the flower display unless they are being grown for their fruits or seedpods.

▲ DRAMA QUEEN
Rhodochiton atrosanguineus, *although perennial, is grown as an annual for the dramatic hue of its flowers and their long, purple-black corollas.*

◄ ELEGANT ARCH
Spanish flag (Ipomoea lobata) *drapes an arch in exotic red blooms that mature through summer to orange and gold.*

through beds among perennials or shrubs. In cooler climates, they are superb for decorating conservatories, where they add dappled shade as well as jazzy color.

SUPPORTING ANNUAL CLIMBERS

Most annual climbers reach 6–10ft (2–3m) or so, and all are self-supporting. Some, such as morning glories and black-eyed Susan vine (*Thunbergia alata*), have twining stems; sweet peas and eccremocarpus cling with delicate tendrils; and climbing nasturtiums and rhodochiton fasten their leaf stalks around any slender support.

The climbers can be trained up formal supports such as obelisks or pergolas; along a wooden trellis, chain-link fencing, or wires attached to a wall; or through a stake tepee or cylinder of wire netting. Tie in young plants with wire rings or twine until they take hold. For an informal look, push large, branched stems (pea sticks) into the ground to form an attractive thicket.

▲ CHEAP AND CHEERFUL
As well as providing thick cover in weeks, Canary creeper (Tropaeolum peregrinum) *has a mass of small, but pretty, fringed flowers.*

SCENTED ANNUALS AND BIENNIALS

FRAGRANCE IS ALL TOO OFTEN OVERLOOKED in the rush to find spectacular combinations of color. But, from light hints of perfume drifting from a border to headier fragrances pervading the air, scent is the essence of the spring and summer garden. When it comes to scent, annuals and biennials have it in abundance. Fragrant plants also entice beneficial insects such as butterflies and bees to pollinate flowers and contribute to the soothing scene.

FLOWERS AND FOLIAGE

Any annual seed mixtures used in the garden or annual border should include scented plants. A freshly picked bouquet would not be complete without at least a few fragrant blooms. When choosing annuals and biennials for scent, bear in mind that not all forms of a plant are necessarily fragrant: for instance, the white forms of flowering tobacco (*Nicotiana*) are often strongly perfumed, while most other cultivars have little or no scent. Petunias are the same, with blues and purples often more strongly scented than other colors.

In some annuals, such as flowering tobacco and stocks (*Matthiola*), the scent is produced mainly during the evening and at night, making the garden a retreat in which to stroll just before sunset. They are also good placed near windows so that their perfume can drift into the house at night.

A few annuals and biennials are not noted for their flowers but are still prized because of the power of their perfume; mignonette (*Reseda odorata*) is one such plant, and it is intoxicatingly sweet.

Of course, not all plants in the annual garden have scented flowers. Some have leaves that are aromatic, especially when they are bruised. These are best grown in containers or near paths so that they are regularly brushed against – try scented-leaved geraniums (*Pelargonium*), or, for a more pungent scent, marigolds (*Tagetes*).

▲ EVENING PERFUME
Cultivars of Matthiola incana *are grown as annuals and release a strong scent at dusk.*

► SWEET AND LOW
Grow sweet alyssum, here Lobularia maritima *Easter Bonnet Series, near a path to enjoy its sweet scent.*

ATTRACTING WILDLIFE

Scented annuals and biennials are some of the best plants for attracting wildlife, especially insects and birds, into a garden. The two most important attributes a flower needs to entice insects are scent and color. The sheer volume of fragrant, colorful flowers borne by annuals and biennials, especially old "cottage-garden" species such as honesty (*Lunaria annua*) and

> Day-flying moths visit petunias; night-flying moths like *Nicotiana*

phlox, makes them beacons for insects. Bees are attracted particularly to blue and yellow, while moths go for white.

As well as scent, flowers that produce plenty of pollen, especially large daisies, are particularly appealing to beetles and beneficial flies, including hoverflies. Having more insects in the garden draws in other wildlife such as birds and small mammals, making the garden a true haven for all.

▲ BEE MAGNET
Two-lipped flowers, such as those of the annual clary (Salvia viridis) *are good for bringing the soothing buzz of bees into the summer garden.*

◀ SPRING INVITATION
The poached-egg plant (Limnanthes douglasii) *attracts early butterflies and bees into the spring garden with its rich offer of sweet nectar.*

PLANTING PLANS AND STYLES

CHOOSING A STYLE OF PLANTING

ANNUALS AND BIENNIALS ARE EXCELLENT for producing quick color in the garden in a range of styles. They can be impressive on their own or can be worked in among more permanent plants but are best when used in harmony with the surrounding planting style. Most need a sunny position, or one in part shade and are usually unfussy about soil type, provided it is well drained. The following pages demonstrate planting ideas for beds, borders, and containers.

ANNUALS AND BIENNIALS IN BORDERS

The traditional way to use annuals and biennials is to devote an entire border or bed to them and create a dazzling display of form and color in the spring and summer months. They remain an essential element of cottage gardening, where plants of various shapes, heights, and colors intermingle in informal borders with complete abandon. If you do not have room for a border that will be bare for part of the year, try adding a blaze of seasonal texture and color by using annuals and biennials as space-fillers in herbaceous borders and among shrubs. They can also be used to charming effect in new gardens, while more permanent plantings establish.

◄ BLUE MOOD
Warm colors used in a limited palette and varying forms can look bold without being busy. Here, the golden mopheads of coreopsis and marigolds meander through drifts of tall blue and white salvia spikes and dainty mauve verbenas.

◄ SUMMER BORDER *Annuals bring a medley of hot colors to liven up the permanent planting.*

THE ANNUAL BORDER

This summer border is devoted to annuals sown directly in a sunny, sheltered site. The plants are stepped from the yew hedge down to the front, where blue anchusas and convolvulus vie with vibrant eschscholzias. Behind them, white rain daisies compete with delicate poppies and nigellas and papery bracteantha heads for grace. At the back, tall consolida spikes and refined pink agrostemma contrast with white lavatera and brazen rudbeckia.

PLANTING PLAN

1 *Agrostemma githago* 'Milas', 28–32in (70–80cm) tall
2 *Rudbeckia hirta*, 28–36in (70–90cm) tall
3 *Lavatera trimestris* 'Mont Blanc', 24–32in (60–80cm)
4 *Consolida ajacis* Imperial Series 36–48in (90–120cm)
5 *Dimorphotheca pluvialis*, 8–12in (20–30cm) tall
6 *Bracteantha bracteata*, 32–36in (80–90cm) tall
7 *Papaver rhoeas* Shirley Series, 24–28in (60–70cm) tall
8 *Nigella damascena* Persian Jewels Series, 18in (45cm)
9 *Anchusa capensis* 'Blue Angel', 8in (20cm) tall
10 *Eschscholzia californica*, 12in (30cm) tall
11 *Convolvulus tricolor* 'Royal Ensign', 8–12in (20–30cm)

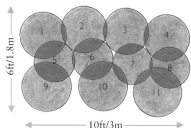

6ft/1.8m

10ft/3m

Rudbeckia hirta has stiff, leafy stems and bold yellow daisies with conical purple-brown centers. It is a good plant for cutting.

Agrostemma githago 'Milas', a corn cockle, bears deep plum-pink flowers on slender, silky-gray stems in early and midsummer.

Dimorphotheca pluvialis, or rain daisy, is easy to grow and has glistening white flowers flushed violet beneath.

Anchusa capensis 'Blue Angel', or Cape alkanet, with its enchanting mass of small, brilliant blue flowers, is an excellent bee plant.

Bracteantha bracteata, or strawflower, has papery everlasting flowers that continue well into autumn and are ideal for drying.

*ESCHSCHOLZIA
CALIFORNICA*
*California poppies begin to
dazzle in early summer;
regular deadheading prolongs
the show well into autumn.*

MORE CHOICES

TALL (over 36in/90cm)
Atriplex hortensis
Cosmos bipinnatus
Malope trifida

MEDIUM
(12–36in/30–90cm)
Antirrhinum majus
Borago officinalis
Chrysanthemum carinatum

Echium vulgare
Gypsophila elegans
Reseda odorata

SMALL (below 12in/30cm)
Calendula officinalis
Iberis umbellata
Layia platyglossa
Linum grandiflorum
Lobelia erinus

Lavatera trimestris '**Mont
Blanc**' forms a compact bush,
unfurling a succession of
virginal white, mallowlike
blooms from summer to
autumn.

Consolida ajacis, or larkspur,
sends up stiff stems of dense
flower spikes in hues of blue,
white, pink, purple, and red; all
are good for cutting and drying.

Nigella damascena **Persian Jewels
Series**, or love-in-a-mist, is an old-
fashioned favorite, with its
feathery foliage, white, blue, and
pink flowers, and pretty seedpods.

CONVOLVULUS TRICOLOR
*'Royal Ensign' is a non-
climbing, bushy bindweed.
Each flower opens in sun and
lasts one day, but many more
appear through summer.*

Papaver rhoeas **Shirley Series** is a delightful
selection of corn poppies, mostly in pastel
shades of pink, rose, orange, and mauve.

A MIXED BORDER

In this informal herbaceous border, annuals and biennials intermingle easily with perennials. Tall spikes of verbascums and biennial foxgloves soar through bold clumps of perennial bellflowers and Shasta daisies.

Below, clouds of annual eschscholzias, centaureas, linums, and lobelias drift between perennial achilleas, bergenias, salvias, and sedums to lift the border with seasonal color. A pyramid of blue morning glories adds a final flourish.

LINUM GRANDIFLORUM '*Rubrum*', *an annual flax, has delicate wandlike stems and eye-catching flowers that last all summer.*

Digitalis purpurea, the common foxglove, has tall spikes of purple, bee-beloved flowers. Watch for abundant self-sown seedlings.

Sedum spectabile, or showy stone-crop, forms a succulent mound of gray-green foliage, evergreen in milder areas. Its pink or purple flowers appear in late summer and are irresistible to butterflies.

Achillea filipendulina 'Gold Plate', a yarrow, bears its flattened flowerheads on stiff stems; they are long-lasting and excellent for drying.

Salvia × superba is a perennial sage. It forms clumps of upright stems bearing spikes of long-lasting, deep blue flowers.

Lobelia 'Crystal Palace' is a low and bushy annual. It is popular for edging a border because it flowers from early summer into autumn.

Eschscholzia lobbii is a dainty California poppy, making low mounds of delicate, ferny foliage adorned with masses of small, satin yellow poppies.

Centaurea cyanus, or annual cornflower, is valued for its frilled flowers in shades of pink, purple, blue, and white; use a dwarfer form for the front of the border.

PLANTING PLAN

1 *Verbascum chaixii*, 39–52in (100–130cm) tall
2 *Achillea filipendulina* 'Gold Plate', 39in (100cm)
3 *Digitalis purpurea*, 39–54in (100–140cm) tall
4 *Ipomoea tricolor* 'Heavenly Blue', 6–10ft (2–3m)
5 *Lavatera trimestris*, 28–36in (70–90cm) tall
6 *Salvia* × *superba*, 32–36in (80–90cm) tall
7 *Sedum spectabile*, 16–20in (40–50cm) tall
8 *Campanula persicifolia*, 32–36in (80–90cm) tall
9 *Centaurea cyanus*, 2–3ft (60–90cm) tall
10 *Leucanthemum* × *superbum*, 36–39in (90–100cm)
11 *Lobelia* 'Crystal Palace', 4–8in (10–20cm) tall
12 *Eschscholzia lobbii*, 6in (15cm) tall
13 *Linum grandiflorum* 'Rubrum', 18in (45cm) tall
14 *Bergenia* 'Silberlicht', 12–16in (30–40cm) tall

6ft/1.7m

9ft/2.8m

Campanula persicifolia has white or blue bells from early to late summer if deadheaded.

Verbascum × *chaixii*, a perennial mullein grown as a biennial, has spires of saucer-shaped, clear yellow flowers rising from coarse, gray basal rosettes of leaves.

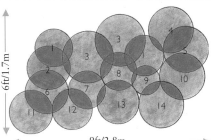

IPOMOEA TRICOLOR *'Heavenly Blue', a morning glory, easily climbs to 10ft (3m) and requires a minimum of 41°F (5°C).*

Lavatera trimestris, an annual in the mallow family, unfurls a succession of silky, pink or white, funnel-shaped blooms all summer long.

MORE CHOICES

TALL (over 36in/90cm)
Ricinus communis
Tithonia rotundifolia

MEDIUM
(12–36in/30–90cm)
Scabiosa atropurpurea
Tanacetum parthenium

SMALL (below 12in/30cm)
Linaria maroccana
Phacelia campanularia

Leucanthemum × *superbum*, the cheery Shasta daisy, bears yellow-centered white daisies that are excellent for cutting.

Bergenia 'Silberlicht' has pink sprays of flowers in the spring, but its chief value lies in its bold, leathery, evergreen leaves.

FORMAL BEDDING

T HE DISCIPLINE OF FORMAL BEDDING forms a stark contrast to the informality of the annual or mixed border. Traditionally, large beds are filled with clearly delineated blocks of massed annuals and short-lived perennials, in simple geometric designs or more complex patterns and knots, to create a fresh design each year. The planting plan on the next page follows the principles of clean lines and blocks of single colors but on a scale suitable for smaller gardens.

CREATING A FORMAL STYLE

Formal designs are best in an open, sunny, but not exposed position where they can be appreciated from all sides. The soil also needs to be well drained yet moisture-retentive. Many modern annuals lend themselves to formal bedding, because they are uniform in shape and vibrant in color. The dwarf, compact cultivars are ideal, as well as those with a long flowering season. Large, bold flowers or foliage can be partnered with smaller types in similar or contrasting colors. Some entrancing effects can also be created using blends of muted color. Bear in mind that formal bedding is most effective if all the plants reach their peak at the same time.

MAKING A FORMAL BED
• Draw the design to scale on graph paper – avoid making it too complicated.
• Mark out the chosen pattern on the ground using stakes and string, or sand.
• Choose plants for any permanent boundary with care; they must remain reasonably small and withstand regular clipping.
• Transplant annuals into the bed, rather than sowing them directly.
• Remember to use foliage plants as well as those with good flower colors or forms.
• Trim and deadhead plants regularly to keep the design looking neat and clearly defined.
• Make sure the bed never dries out, which would tend to make the growth uneven.

◀ FOCUS ON FORM
Rounded banks of Leucanthemum 'Show Star' edge a formal bed dominated by the flamboyant blooms and foliage of cannas. Spikes of annual salvia hug their flanks as the red of the cannas is echoed by mixed geraniums in neighboring beds.

◀ CARPET BEDDING Senecio cineraria *and* Begonia semperflorens *form swirls of silver and red.*

A FORMAL BED

Here a square design is enclosed by dwarf boxwood, neatly clipped for a strong line, and surrounded by gravel. The centerpiece is a castor bean with large, bronze leaves that effectively sets off the drooping tassels of amaranthus.

Around them, opposing triangles of violet salvias and pink geraniums jostle for attention. Low edging strips of golden marigolds and salmon-pink impatiens end in corner blocks of cool blue lobelias and ageratums.

PLANTING PLAN

1 *Buxus sempervirens* 'Suffruticosa', 3ft (1m) tall
2 *Ageratum houstonianum* 'Adriatic', 6–8in (15–20cm) tall
3 *Impatiens walleriana* Super Elfin Series, 6–8in (15–20cm)
4 *Lobelia* 'Cambridge Blue', 6in (15cm) tall
5 *Pelargonium* 'Multibloom Pink', 12–16in (30–40cm) tall
6 *Tagetes* 'Golden Gem', 8in (20cm) tall
7 *Amaranthus caudatus*, 2–3ft (60–90cm) tall
8 *Ricinus communis*, 39–48in (100–120cm) tall
9 *Salvia splendens* Cleopatra Series, 12in (30cm) tall

10ft/3m

10ft/3m

AMARANTHUS CAUDATUS
This dramatic plant has coarse leaves and splendid, pendent tassels of blood red flowers, hence its common name, love-lies-bleeding.

Salvia splendens **Cleopatra Series** is a violet-flowered selection of scarlet sage. It makes a neat, bushy plant and flowers all summer.

RECOMMENDED HEDGING PLANTS

The best hedging plants for use in formal bedding designs are dwarf forms that are able to tolerate regular clipping. Evergreens are most often used to provide a permanent framework in which to plant new bedding each year. The hedge may take three or four years after planting to reach the desired height and shape.

Buxus sempervirens
'Suffruticosa'
Lavandula angustifolia
(compact forms)

Lonicera nitida
Santolina chamaecyparissus
Satureja montana
Teucrium chamaedrys
Teucrium fruticans
Thymus × *citriodorus*
Thymus vulgaris

Ricinus communis, the castor bean, is a branching shrub often grown as an annual specimen plant. It bears impressive, large, lobed foliage in bronze-red, purple, or deep green.

Lobelia 'Cambridge Blue' is a popular plant for bedding, especially edging, because it forms compact clumps with a profusion of pale blue flowers.

Buxus sempervirens 'Suffruticosa', like all boxwood, is a slow-growing evergreen, ideal for hedging. It can reach 3ft (1m), but it can be kept to half that height by clipping it twice a year.

Tagetes 'Golden Gem' is a Signet marigold, producing flowers that appear in profusion.

Pelargonium 'Multibloom Pink', one of many kinds of geranium, is widely grown as an annual, flowering quickly and lavishly from seed.

AGERATUM HOUSTONIANUM 'Adriatic', and other dwarf forms of the floss flower, make neat little domes of foliage that are smothered in powderpuff flowers for many weeks.

Impatiens walleriana, the common impatiens, has many fine dwarf forms, including this one with showy, salmon-pink blooms.

PLANTING IN CONTAINERS

MANY ANNUALS, BIENNIALS, AND PERENNIALS grown as annuals thrive in containers. They are ideal for small gardens, creating focal points in courtyards and on patios, filling gaps in summer borders, and adorning walls and windowsills. As the plants in one container fade, another can replace it, keeping a display at the height of perfection for many months. A variety of ideas for pretty plantings in containers are shown on the following pages.

CHOOSING APPROPRIATE CONTAINERS

The choice of container is very much a personal one. A huge variety is now available in simple or ornate styles and in a wide range of colors, including those made of concrete, pottery, terracotta, plastic, metal, and wood. As well as pots and barrels, make use of wall space by filling hanging and wall baskets. Another option is a flower pillar or column that can be planted up with dozens of plants to create a spectacular display of bloom in a small space. For those without a garden, a windowbox, properly secured, can sustain a surprisingly large variety of plants.

When choosing containers, consider how they complement the colors and textures of the plants and the environment in which they will be placed. If grouping containers, do not use too many different styles and colors; otherwise, the effect will be fussy.

PRACTICAL TIPS
• Choose containers that are large and deep enough to allow the plants' roots to develop.
• Smaller containers dry out more rapidly and require more frequent watering.
• Place larger containers in position before filling them – they can become very heavy.
• Choose a moisture-retentive soil mix, such as a soil-based potting mix.
• Add moisture-retentive granules and slow-release fertilizers to keep the plants in vigorous growth for as long as possible.
• Locate containers in a sheltered position in sun or part shade (impatiens flower best in dappled shade).
• Keep drainage holes free from blockage by raising the container off the ground by 6in (15cm); half-bricks are ideal for this.
• Ensure that baskets, pillars, and other wall-mounted containers are securely anchored.

◀ SIMPLE CHARM
The more delicate delights among annuals, such as these pansies, Viola 'Sorbet Yellow Frost', *are perhaps best enjoyed planted individually in pots, unhindered by gaudier plants.*

◀ CASCADE OF BLOOM *Baskets and pots brim over with lobelia, impatiens, and geraniums.*

A GROUP OF CONTAINERS

With regular fertilizing and dead-heading, this display, in pots ranging in size from 9–30in (23–75cm), will last until autumn. The focal point of the group is formed by thunbergias clambering up a stake tripod. More height and volume come from slender nicotianas and lush geraniums. Lobelias, suteras, nasturtiums, and verbenas create more variations of form and color while softening the hard edges of the containers.

Thunbergia alata is a free-flowering, twining climber. Its flowers may be white, cream, or orange and always have black eyes, hence its name, black-eyed Susan vine.

Lobelia 'Sapphire' has slender, trailing stems and profuse, two-lipped flowers of deep sapphire-blue.

Scaevola aemula 'New Wonder' is like lobelia but more spreading than trailing, with larger and coarser blue flowers.

NICOTIANA 'LIME GREEN'
This flowering tobacco has flowers of an unusual yellow-green, which is a superb foil for purples and reds. They also release a wonderful fragrance at night.

Tropaeolum majus 'Hermine Grashoff' is a nasturtium with tumbling foliage and scented, showy, double orange-red flowers. It cannot be raised from seed; take stem-tip cuttings instead.

Sutera grandiflora 'Sea Mist' has delicate, spreading and trailing stems and a profusion of tiny flowers, perfect for tumbling over the edge of a container.

PLANTING PLAN

1 *Nicotiana* 'Lime Green', 20–24in (50–60cm)
2 *Tropaeolum majus* 'Hermine Grashoff',
  8–12in (20–30cm) tall
3 *Sutera grandiflora* 'Sea Mist', 6–12in
  (15–30cm) tall
4 *Thunbergia alata*, 6–10ft (2–3m) tall
5 *Lobelia* 'Sapphire', 8in (20cm) tall
6 *Scaevola aemula* 'New Wonder', 8–12in
  (20–30cm) tall
7 *Gazania* Daybreak Series, 8in (20cm) tall
8 *Impatiens* Super Elfin Series, 8–20in (20–50cm) tall
9 *Pelargonium* 'Multibloom Pink', 16–24in (40–60cm) tall
10 *Mimulus* Malibu Series, 8–20in (20–50cm) tall
11 *Verbena* 'Imagination', 8–12in (20–30cm) tall
12 *Torenia fournieri* 'Blue Moon', 8–16in (20–40cm) tall

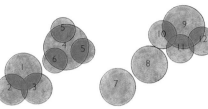

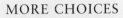

MORE CHOICES

BUSHY
Browallia speciosa
Catharanthus roseus
Heliotropium arborescens

TRAILING
Petunia integrifolia
Sanvitalia procumbens

FOLIAGE
Helichrysum petiolare
Solenostemon scutellarioides

Mimulus Malibu Series, or monkey flower, thrives in moist soil mix. Its cream, yellow, orange, pink, or red trumpets are often nicely spotted.

Pelargonium 'Multibloom Pink' is one of a number of modern bushy, very free-flowering geraniums, perfect for all containers.

Gazania Daybreak Series is a striking, tufted plant with daisies in pink, white, orange, yellow, or bronze that open in sun.

Torenia 'Blue Moon' is a bushy annual with two-toned blue and purple flowers that persist into autumn.

Verbena 'Imagination' has a semitrailing habit, producing bright clusters of blooms in deep violet-blue.

Impatiens Super Elfin Series, a form of the popular impatiens, is perfect for filling a container by itself, with its hues of red, pink, orange, mauve, or white.

WINDOWBOX AND HANGING BASKET

Like all containers, these require daily watering and regular deadheading and feeding to keep the plants at their best. Special fastenings are now available for lowering hanging baskets to make access easier. Never be afraid to pack a container full of annuals, especially hanging baskets; they rarely look good when underplanted. Hanging baskets look lush brimming with a single, vigorous subject, but windowboxes are more effective with a mix of plants.

PLANTING PLAN FOR WINDOWBOX

1 *Sutera grandiflora* 'Knysna Hills', 12in (30cm)
2 *Exacum affine*, 8–12in (20–30cm) tall
3 *Torenia fournieri* 'Blue Moon', 16in (40cm)
4 *Tagetes* 'Tangerine Gem', 8in (20cm) tall
5 *Lobelia* 'Snowball', 8in (20cm) tall
6 *Brachyscome iberidifolia*, 16in (40cm) tall
7 *Verbena* 'Tapien Pink', 8in (20cm) tall
8 *Begonia semperflorens* hybrids, 12in (30cm)
9 *Impatiens walleriana* Tempo Series, 9in (23cm) tall

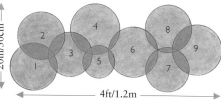

20in/50cm

4ft/1.2m

Tagetes 'Tangerine Gem', a Signet marigold, is a sturdy, pungent-leaved annual with long-lasting daisies of bright tangerine-orange.

Lobelia 'Snowball' is a bushy lobelia with pale green foliage and a mass of dashing white flowers.

Exacum affine, or Persian violet, is most often grown as a houseplant but looks just as good in a summer windowbox. It has bright green, fleshy foliage and purple-blue flowers with bold yellow stamens.

Torenia fournieri 'Blue Moon', a wishbone flower, is also grown as summer bedding or a houseplant.

Sutera 'Knysna Hills', the purple glory plant, with its spreading to semitrailing stems and free-flowering habit, is ideal for softening hard edges.

Petunia Surfinia Series are ideal for hanging baskets: they have a markedly trailing habit, and the blooms are long-lasting, produced in abundance over a long season, and remarkably weather-resistant. A similar effect can be created with ivy-leaved geraniums.

Brachyscome iberidifolia, or Swan River daisy, is a delightful, spreading to half-trailing annual with finely dissected foliage and a myriad of small daisies, each with a soft yellow center.

MORE CHOICES

HANGING BASKETS
Impatiens walleriana
Ipomoea batatas
Lobelia erinus
Solenostemon (Coleus)
Thunbergia alata
Verbena

WINDOWBOXES
Capsicum annuum
Felicia amelloides
Impatiens New Guinea Group
Pelargonium (trailing and ivy-leaved types)
Petunia
Rosa
Sanvitalia procumbens
Scaevola aemula
Senecio cineraria
Tradescantia fluminensis

Begonia semperflorens is a succulent, bushy annual with "sugared" flowers in shades of pink, red, or white from summer to autumn.

Impatiens walleriana is the familiar impatiens. It thrives in sun or part shade and is one of the very best container plants. This Tempo Series has flowers in a range of colors, except true blue and yellow.

Verbena 'Tapien Pink' is a spreading plant with feathery leaves and flat clusters of rich pink flowers. It flowers freely over a long season.

LOOKING AFTER YOUR PLANTS

THE KEY TO SUCCESS

ANNUALS AND BIENNIALS are generally rather undemanding plants, but to get the most out of them, planting and care are important. It is well worth spending time on preparing the soil before sowing or planting, and choosing appropriate plants for the soil type and site. You will be rewarded with a succession of vigorous flowers from late spring through autumn.

PREPARING THE GROUND

A border full of colorful annuals is an exciting and gratifying sight in any garden. To achieve this is not difficult, as long as the site is appropriate to the plants, the soil is well prepared, and the plants are healthy. Select a site that meets the light needs of the plants, in soil that is not too rich – most annuals thrive in average, well-drained soil. Soil preparation is best tackled in autumn, if practical, and completed over a few days to make the task less onerous.

SOIL PREPARATION

• Clear the area of pernicious weeds, such as bindweed, thistles, goutweed, or quackgrass, if necessary.
• If the soil is in good condition, fork it over. If the soil is compacted, dig it to a depth of a spade's blade.
• Remove all pieces of weeds, then rake level.
• Add a slow-release fertilizer to poor soils.
• Inspect the site regularly and weed if needed.

Sturdy, bushy growth

Unbalanced growth

BUYING A PLANT
When buying young plants for bedding, take care to choose vigorous, healthy plants with good, deep green foliage and no sign of pests or diseases. Avoid any plants with yellowing leaves, stunted growth, dry, weedy soil mix, or potbound roots – they almost never thrive or flower well.

HEALTHY PLANT

UNHEALTHY PLANT

◀ PERFECT PARTNERS *Tall, spiky foxgloves soar above the large, crimson bowls of opium poppies.*

SOWING ANNUAL SEED UNDER COVER

Raising plants from seed to flowering can be one of the most rewarding experiences in gardening. Annuals are ideal for the new or impatient gardener who wants quick and colorful results, because they often mature and flower within weeks of sowing. In temperate climates, seeds of many annuals are best sown under cover in late winter into spring, so that the seedlings may be planted out once all danger of frost has passed.

SOWING INTO TRAYS

Use good-sized seed trays when sowing fairly large quantities of seed. Always use clean containers and fresh, sterilized seed-starting mix to lessen disease problems. If the soil mix is too coarse, screen or sieve it first to get a finely textured surface on which to sow. Once the seed is sown, the ideal place for them is in a greenhouse or cold frame, but a bright windowsill is fine, if it is out of direct sun.

1 Firm the mix in the tray with another tray, a wooden presser, or your hand, to ½in (1cm) below the rim. Water well; allow to drain.

2 Sow seed thinly over the entire surface and, if the seeds are large, add a thin layer of mix or similar fine material to cover them. Label.

3 Cover the tray with plastic wrap or glass to keep the mix moist. Put in a light place, not in full sun. Uncover when the seeds germinate.

SOWING INTO POTS

For smaller amounts of seed, you can use clay, plastic, or degradable pots. The method of sowing is the same as with trays (*see above*). Do not overly firm the mix or sow too thickly: this will result in crowded, spindly seedlings and runs the risk of damping off, which can quickly kill an entire potful. Always remember to label each pot to avoid confusion later.

USING VERMICULITE
Covering seed with a thin layer of vermiculite or perlite keeps the seeds moist and protects them when watered.

Space large seeds evenly

DEGRADABLE POT
Sow 2 or 3 large seeds in a degradable pot. Thin to one seedling. Plant out in the pot to avoid disturbing the roots.

LOOKING AFTER SEEDLINGS

To develop healthily, seedlings need bright light and moisture. Light-starved seedlings (*see right*) rarely make vigorous plants, but they can also become damaged in strong sunlight. They must also never be allowed to dry out. If the soil mix drains freely, overwatering should not be a problem.

Do not let seedlings linger too long in seed containers, because they will become too crowded and develop extensive root systems that will be difficult to untangle when they are transplanted (*below*). The best time to transplant is when they have one or two true leaves; these develop after the first leaf or pair of leaves (cotyledons).

Long, drawn stems

PROVIDING LIGHT
Once seeds have germinated, it is important to ensure that the seedlings receive even, bright light. If not, they will become pale and drawn (etiolated). Turn containers on windowsills regularly so that the seedlings are not drawn to one side.

1 **Lift seedlings carefully** from the soil mix, using your finger or a pencil. Hold each seedling by its tiny leaves; if the fragile stem is damaged, the seedling will probably die.

2 **Insert the seedlings** in containers of fresh soil mix, spacing them evenly in rows and making a hole large enough to take each seedling's roots. Water with a fine spray.

USING CELL TRAYS

Cell trays (also called cell packs) come in many sizes and a variety of materials, but particularly plastic. They have an advantage over traditional trays and pots in that seedlings are disturbed as little as possible, each developing in its own compartment until it is ready to be potted up or planted out. Seeds can be sown directly into small cells, or seedlings can be transplanted into larger cells. Cells can dry out quickly, so water carefully.

SEEDLING PLUG PLANT
It is easy to keep the root ball of a seedling intact when lifting it from a cell.

SOWING ANNUAL SEED OUTDOORS

MOST ANNUALS, ESPECIALLY THE MORE COLD-RESISTANT kinds, are ideal for direct sowing outdoors. With little effort, large areas can be sown to create a plenty of color in a short time. Any decent, well-drained soil is fine, but soil preparation (*see p.45*) is the key to achieving a good display. Do not use fertilizers or organic manures – they make annuals too soft, lanky, and leafy – but add an organic fertilizer if annuals have been sown in the area before.

BROADCASTING SEED

Scattering seed is quicker than sowing it in drills (*see facing page*) but has the disadvantage of not allowing any hoeing between rows of seedlings or young plants. To broadcast seed, rake the prepared ground to a fine tilth. Scatter the seed as evenly as possible, then lightly rake over the sown area to cover the seed.

SOWING THE SEED

COVERING THE SEED

MARKING OUT ANNUAL BORDERS

Annuals are most effective when sown in large blocks. To achieve this, mark out the ground, once it has been prepared and raked, by using pegs and strings, scoring the ground with a stake, or pouring lines of sand. Make each plot within the border fairly large; broad, overlapping sweeps are more effective than small ones.

MARKING OUT THE GROUND
Trickle lines of sharp sand or pour it from a bottle; it is easily seen and "erased." Draw out one large area for each type of seed.

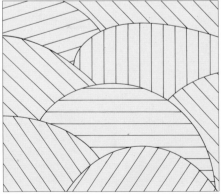

PLAN OF A PLOT FOR SOWING
Drills in adjacent plots should run in different directions. Mark them out with a stake or the point of a hoe, 4–5in (10–12cm) apart.

SOWING INTO DRILLS IN BORDERS

It helps to have made a rough plan on paper before starting to sow into the marked plots, so that you sow annuals of complementary heights and colors in adjacent blocks. The names of each annual can also be written on the plan for future reference. If the soil is very dry, water the drills lightly before sowing. Old annual seed can be sown more thickly than usual, because it tends to germinate erratically.

1 **Trickle the seeds** evenly and thinly from your hand along the bottom of the drill. Very fine seed can be sown directly from the packet. Try not to sow the seed too thickly.

2 **Cover the seed** by carefully brushing the soil across the drill. Firm the soil gently, then water the drill using a watering can with a fine nozzle to avoid disturbing the seed.

3 **When the seedlings first appear,** they may look rather sparse, but they will soon fill in to form dense drifts. Check the rows regularly; hoe off any weeds between them.

4 **Thin the seedlings,** if necessary, to 2–2½in (5–6cm) apart, or more for large annuals. Pull out unwanted seedlings while firming the soil around those that are to be kept.

SOWING SEEDS SINGLY

Climbers such as morning glories, as well as annuals such as sunflowers, have fairly large seeds that can be sown individually. Make small holes in the prepared soil with your finger or a stick and place one or two seeds in each, then cover with soil. The advantage of double sowing is that if one seed should fail, the other may germinate. If both seeds germinate, remove the weaker seedling. When sowing climbing annuals, place the supports, such as pea sticks or a tepee, in position before sowing the seed.

SOWING SEEDS BY A STAKE TEPEE
Sow two seeds at the base of each stake; thin out the weaker seedling at the 4-leaf stage.

PLANTING ANNUALS

ANNUALS RAISED IN SEED TRAYS, POTS, OR CELLS will need to be transplanted into the garden or containers. For the hardiest annuals, any time in spring will do, but for other types, it is best to wait until all danger of frost has passed; this may not be until early summer in some areas. In such cases, keep the plants growing strongly by potting them on regularly into fresh soil mix.

PLANTING NEW ANNUALS IN A BED

As for seed sowing, it is crucial to prepare the soil (*see p.45*) before planting annuals. Ideally, the soil should be warm and moist, especially for tender bedding annuals. Avoid planting into cold or very wet soils. Remove young plants from their containers with care to avoid damaging their delicate root systems, and plant out evenly spaced.

PLANTING OUT

PLANTING A WINDOWBOX

A windowbox brings the garden almost into the house. Never be afraid to put in plenty of plants; sparsely planted containers look decidedly lackluster. Before planting, water the plants well and decide how to arrange them. Contrast bold annuals with dainty ones, erect plants with trailing types. Fill the windowbox with moist potting mix to within ¾in (2cm) of the rim; water-retentive granules can be added to the soil mix to keep it moist. Feed the planted windowbox regularly with liquid fertilizer to keep the plants growing healthily.

1 **Knock each plant** gently from its pot, supporting the root ball at the base of the stem. Tease the roots out a little.

2 **Plant the larger** subjects first. Make sure the crowns of the plants are ½in (1cm) below the rim, to allow for watering.

3 **Finish with trailing plants** at the front, firming each in gently. If needed, add more soil mix. Level the surface and water well.

PLANTING A HANGING BASKET

Generally, a mixture of bushy and trailing annuals works well in a hanging basket, although they can be effective if planted with only one star performer, such as impatiens. Once planted, baskets should be left for a few weeks under cover to establish before being placed outdoors, especially if tender annuals are used. The best site for a basket is in a part of the garden sheltered from drying winds.

A PLANTED BASKET
Plant trailing and spreading annuals up the sides and around the edge, and bushy, upright ones in the center, to form a globe of bloom.

BASKET LINERS

Open baskets, whether plastic or metal, need to be lined to hold the soil and conserve water. Sphagnum moss is the traditional lining material, but many other materials are available for use and work almost as well. Modern materials include foam, felt, and coir liners. Some are precut to the correct basket shape and size. Additional moisture retention can be gained by mixing water-retentive granules into the soil mix. Do not add too many; otherwise, the soil mix will expand out of the basket like an over-risen cake.

FOAM LINER

1 **Support the basket** on a large pot. Press the liner into the basket and trim off any excess. Fill the lower third of the basket with potting mix and water-retentive granules.

2 **Cut cross slits** in the side of the liner with a sharp knife to allow plants to be pushed through the liner, roots first. If moss is used, push holes through with your fingers.

3 **Ease trailing plants** through the slits, trying not to damage the roots unduly. Fill in the basket with more soil mix, plant up the top of the basket, firm gently, and water well.

BIENNIALS

SOME OF THE LOVELIEST PLANTS grown in our gardens are biennials; that is, plants that flower in their second year from seed, then die, having first set seed. Biennials are rather awkward plants, taking up precious space for their first year without producing any flowers. However, many have interesting leaf rosettes and sit comfortably in a mixed border or cottage garden, rather than a traditional annual border, which is cleared at the end of the season.

GROWING BIENNIALS

Biennial seed may be sown in late winter or any time up to early summer. Many can be raised under cover and treated like bedding annuals for planting out in early summer where they are to flower. A better option is to set aside a small plot for the biennials so that they do not need to be transplanted into their flowering positions until autumn; a part of the vegetable garden is ideal.

Sow biennials in a prepared seedbed in late spring or early summer, then transplant them into a nursery bed until autumn (*see below*). Alternatively, sow seed sparingly in drills at the nursery-bed spacings, thin the seedlings, and grow on. Place netting over them to keep off birds and cats (*see p.54*), and keep them watered. When seedlings emerge, protect them from slugs and snails.

CHOICE BIENNIALS

Most of these biennials are easy to raise from seed, and many self-sow freely.

Bellis perennis, English daisy
Campanula medium, Canterbury bell
Dianthus barbatus, sweet William
Digitalis purpurea, foxglove
Eryngium giganteum, Miss Wilmott's ghost
Erysimum cheiri, wallflower
Lunaria annua, honesty
Meconopsis betonicifolia, Himalayan poppy
Myosotis sylvatica, forget-me-not
Oenothera biennis, evening primrose
Onorpordum acanthium, Scotch thistle
Smyrnium perfoliatum, perfoliate Alexander
Verbascum bombyciferum, Turkish mullein

1 **As soon as the seedlings** are 2–3in (5–8cm) tall, lift them from the seedbed using a hand fork. Retain as much soil around the roots as you possibly can.

2 **Plant out** the seedlings 6–8in (15–20cm) apart, in rows 8–12in (20–30cm) apart, in a nursery bed. Allow the roots plenty of room. Firm in gently and water thoroughly.

3 **In the autumn,** lift the young plants and transfer them to their final positions. (If the nursery bed is dry, water it well, several hours before digging up the plants.)

OVERWINTERING BIENNIALS

Most biennials are quite hardy. However, a few dislike excessive winter moisture and will benefit from a plastic or glass cover. Both Himalayan poppies and Turkish mulleins fall into this category. Whereas most biennials remain evergreen through the winter, often forming a symmetrical leaf rosette, some, like the Himalayan poppy, wither back to an overwintering bud. A few, like the wallflower, make a bushy plant, even in the first year.

FIRST-YEAR SEEDLINGS
The leaf rosettes of the Canterbury bell are evergreen and send up their flowering stems in the spring of the second year.

TRANSPLANTING SELF-SOWN SEEDLINGS

Many biennials produce quantities of seed and self-sow readily around the garden. Seedlings are often found in the vicinity of the parent plants, although sometimes the seed is blown considerable distances. It is not always easy to distinguish very small, biennial seedlings from those of weeds, so if you want to preserve the biennials, do not weed until all the seedlings have several true, or typical, leaves. You should then be able to recognize them and can either lift and transplant them to other parts of the garden (*see below*) or weed around them, leaving them to replace the parent plants.

1 **In late summer** or early autumn, look for seedlings nestling on the ground close to a mature plant (here a foxglove, *Digitalis purpurea*). Water the ground if it is dry.

2 **Lift the seedlings** gently using a trowel or a hand fork, being careful to keep as much soil as possible around the delicate roots to ensure the seedlings reestablish well.

3 **Replant the seedlings**, at least 12in (30cm) apart, where the plants are to flower the following year. Firm in gently and keep well watered until they are established.

PLANT CARE THROUGH THE SEASON

S EVERAL MEASURES CAN BE TAKEN to ensure even and healthy growth in young
annuals and biennials and to achieve a better crop of bloom. Plants should
be protected from competing weeds and damaging pests and given support if
necessary. Water if the soil becomes too dry. Annuals in containers can be fed
by adding slow-release fertilizer to the soil mix or with liquid fertilizers, but
those in borders do not need feeding unless the soil is very impoverished.

PROTECTION AND SUPPORT

All plants raised under cover should be
hardened off (acclimatized) before being
planted in the open garden. Protection
from pests is needed for vulnerable young
plants. Tall or climbing annuals and
biennials and those with thin stems benefit
from some support, from pea sticks or
cylinders of wire mesh to a trellis.
Whatever you use, put it in place when the
plants are young; it is harder to do
inconspicuously with semimature plants,
especially without damaging them.

HARDENING OFF YOUNG PLANTS
*Before setting out plants grown under cover,
acclimatize them by protecting them from
cold winds or frost with plastic or rowcover.*

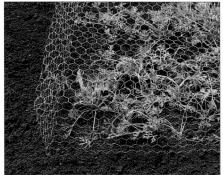

PROTECTION AGAINST PESTS
*Wire or plastic netting placed over young
plants will protect them from cats and birds.
Slug and snail controls may also be necessary.*

PROVIDING SUPPORT
*Pea sticks are ideal for annuals, disappearing
from sight as the plants grow. Place around
young plants, but not too close to their roots.*

TYING IN SUPPORTS
*Support tall annuals
in containers or in
borders by pushing
stakes into the soil
and twining string
around the stakes (see
left). Climbing plants
may need to be
started off by tying in
the shoots loosely
with soft ties that
will not damage the
young growth.*

DEADHEADING

Regular deadheading removes unsightly fading blooms and, more importantly, prolongs the flowering season of many annuals and biennials. This is because plants divert energy from to producing fruits and cease flowering once they have developed mature seedheads. Large flowers are easiest to deadhead, but it is totally impractical to deadhead those with tiny flowers, such as gypsophila. If ornamental fruits or seeds are required, then deadhead plants only lightly or not at all.

▲ SHORT-STEMMED FLOWERS
When each flower (here a petunia) fades, pinch off the stem with your fingers, close to the leaf joint below.

◄ FLOWERS WITH LONG STEMS
These are much easier to deadhead: cut out the stems or flower spike (here a salvia) with pruners or sharp scissors, but be sure to take out the stems close to the first mature leaves below; otherwise, the deadheaded stalks will look unsightly and can allow disease to enter the plant.

END-OF-SEASON TASKS

During the autumn, particularly after the first frost, annuals start to die and look unsightly. At this stage, they are best pulled up and disposed of, either on the compost pile or discarded; if seeding is likely to be a problem, then the latter option is better.

The soil can then be forked or dug over and well-rotted compost, bone meal, or alfalfa worked in at the same time. Annuals can be grown successfully on the same land for many years, provided it does not become infested with perennial weeds.

CLEARING DEAD AND DYING PLANTS
Use a rake to clear the ground methodically from the front of a border to the back. Try to avoid trampling on and compacting the soil, especially if it is quite heavy, such as clay.

WATERING TIPS

• Some annuals and biennials, especially impatiens and petunias, need ample and regular watering. Most, however, need watering only during hot, dry weather.

• Overwatering causes lush, soft growth that is prone to flop over in wind or heavy rain. Plenty of water applied infrequently is far better than watering little and often.

• Apply a rather light, gentle spray over beds to avoid battering down plants, but be sure to give plants enough water.

• If possible, use rainwater gathered in a barrel or recycled water (from the kitchen sink or bathtub) to conserve supplies. Do not use water that contains strong detergents.

GATHERING SEED

Harvesting your own seed can be rewarding – and reduce your seed costs. Annuals and biennials often set seed in abundance, so you can share the seed with other gardeners. Many seeds come true to type, producing seedlings identical to the parent. Seed of hybrids and some named cultivars does not come true, and plants are often inferior; such seed is best discarded. Some annuals and biennials naturally hybridize and give rise to pleasing variations.

EXTRACTING THE SEED

Seed is contained in many types of fruit or seedhead. In the simplest forms, seed is borne in a dry capsule; it can be shaken out or the capsule gently crushed to gather the seed. Some seedheads will fall apart into single-seeded pieces. In the flowerheads of daisies, numerous seeds are embedded in a flattened or cone-shaped disk, and these can be removed fairly readily. The most difficult fruits are those that are sticky or fleshy; it can be quite difficult, messy, and time-consuming to extract the seed.

POPPIES
When the poppy seed capsule is mature, a ring of pores appears at the top and the tiny seeds can be shaken out, like pepper from a shaker. Transfer the seed into small envelopes.

GRASSES
Grass seed is ripe when the flowerheads begin to break up. Pull the head through your hand to sift seed and chaff into a gathering bag. After cleaning it, store seed in a paper bag.

SUNFLOWERS
The seedhead consists of hundreds of seeds partly embedded on the central disk. When the sunflower is dry and brown, the seeds are ripe. Rub them off by hand over clean paper.

HONESTY
Honesty seed pods are flat and oval, with the seeds pressed to a central membrane. Gently peel away the outer husks from each side of the membrane to expose the flat seeds.

PREPARING AND STORING SEED

Remember that seeds are living things: they must be looked after carefully if they are to remain viable until the next year and achieve a good rate of germination. Home-gathered seed should therefore be properly dried, sorted, and stored.

Ripe fruits or seedheads should be completely dry before they are stored, to avoid mold infecting and killing the seed. Often there will be some (or a great deal of) chaff or detritus mixed in with the seed; this will need to be separated out before the seed is stored. Papery seed capsules generally require little preparation and can be stored whole. The seed of fleshy fruits must be removed before the fruits start to rot and become moldy by picking individual seeds out by hand. Wear gloves when preparing seed; some can cause skin allergies, and others are poisonous.

Always store seed in envelopes or boxes; plastic bags increase humidity, so the seed may rot. Make sure that the bags are clearly labeled; otherwise, mixups are certain to occur, however well you think you can distinguish different seeds.

DRYING SEEDS
After gathering fruits and seedheads, place them in open boxes or paper bags. Leave for a day or so in a warm, dry place away from bright light, and shake them occasionally.

SORTING SEEDS FROM CHAFF
Sieves of varying mesh size can be used to rid seeds of unwanted chaff. Place the seeds in the sieve and shake gently; if the sieve is the right size, only the seeds will fall through.

STORING SEEDS
Place clean seed in paper envelopes or packets and label clearly. Store in a cool, dry place away from bright light, such as an airtight container on a lower shelf of a refrigerator.

PRACTICAL TIPS

• Most capsules are ripe when papery and brown; fleshy fruits when they change color. Once plants have flowered, check regularly and gather seeds as soon as they are ripe.

• Reject any fruits or seedheads that show signs of mold or other disease.

• Fine chaff can be kept and sown with seed.

• Label each seed packet with the full plant name and date of gathering.

• Seed of many annuals and biennials can be stored at 34–41°F (1–5°C) for several years.

CALENDULA

AVOIDING PLANT PROBLEMS

A NNUALS AND BIENNIALS ARE, on the whole, remarkably free of pests and diseases in the garden, although young plants may be vulnerable to slugs and aphids. Good garden hygiene, and vigorous plants that are grown in good soil and kept well watered, are more likely to remain healthy and free of pests or diseases. If problems do arise, there is generally no need to resort to noxious chemicals, which often kill indiscriminately (both friend and foe) in the garden.

PREVENTION AND CURE

Encouraging wildlife into the garden keeps many pests at bay, or at least at a level that causes little harm. Some annuals attract beneficial insects, which may help to protect more vulnerable plants such as roses. Birds seek out many insect pests, and it is easy to protect seedbeds or young plants from their foraging by placing netting or black thread over the plants.

Cats can be troublesome, but a variety of devices, including ultrasound alarms and scented pellets, are available. The main pests in the garden are likely to be aphids and slugs or snails. For these, various eco-friendly controls are available.

More problems are likely to occur under cover, especially with the raising of tender annuals. Here scrupulous hygiene is crucial. Always use clean pots or trays and fresh, sterile soil mix. Spider mite (*see below*) and some kinds of scale insect can be controlled biologically by releasing natural predators into the greenhouse.

Regularly inspect your plants, both in the garden and under cover, to spot problems at an early stage, when control is easier. Many pests can be hand-picked. Once they are established, pests and diseases are more difficult to control and may already have inflicted considerable damage to the plants.

▲ SPIDER MITE DAMAGE
These mites are tiny, so the first sign is often brown speckling, then yellowing, of leaves. A humid atmosphere helps keep mites at bay.

BENEFICIAL INSECTS
Lacewings (above) *ladybugs* (right), *and hoverflies are particularly effective at keeping down aphids, one of the more troublesome garden pests. Rather than using any pesticides, encourage these beneficial insects into the garden by growing annuals and biennials that are rich in nectar.*

▶ DAMPING OFF
This fungal disease causes seedlings to collapse suddenly. Avoid it by sowing seed thinly, using sterile, free-draining soil mix in a clean container, and not overwatering the pot.

A CALENDAR OF SEASONAL REMINDERS

WINTER

• Neaten annual beds, removing dead and dying growth for composting or disposal. Take care not to add seedheads to compost piles, because they may germinate where they are not wanted the following year.

• Fork or dig over annual beds (or plots in mixed borders), leaving them bare during the winter so that frost can break down the soil and produce a finer surface by spring.

• Avoid trampling heavier soils, such as clay, especially in wet weather.

• Add bone meal or another slow-release organic fertilizer to enrich the soil.

• Start planning and selecting annuals for the following year; browse in garden centers and seed catalogs before ordering seeds or plants for the spring.

• Draw up sowing or planting plans on paper, thinking about color, height, and form, for the following season.

SPRING

• Start sowing tender annuals under cover in gentle heat and in bright light. Root cuttings of perennials grown as annuals.

• Sow seed of biennials outdoors, and hardier annuals as gap-fillers in mixed borders.

• Outside, clear away any weeds that have appeared, and rake over the ground to level it and to produce a fine tilth.

• Start to sow seed of annuals and biennials outdoors.

• Prick out annuals under cover.

• Thin annuals if necessary.

• Check regularly for any signs of pests or diseases; protect new plants from slugs and aphids, and remove any plants that show signs of pests or disease.

• Begin staking tall or climbing annuals with stakes, pea sticks, metal rings, or wire netting.

• Begin planting up containers for summer displays; grow on in a frost-free place.

USING CLOCHES
Annuals and biennials that have been directly sown in the garden can be protected from cold and frost under a cloche until the weather settles.

SUMMER

• Place plants outside and harden them off once frost danger has passed.

• Finish staking, being careful not to damage the young growth.

• Plant out annuals in the garden and in containers.

• Fertilize containers (once the plants have become established) if the soil mix does not contain a long-term fertilizer.

• Water containers daily and young plants in dry periods.

• Weed regularly and inspect plants for signs of pests or diseases; control problems if needed.

• Regular, frequent deadheading will help prolong the flowering season. If seed is desired, stop deadheading while there are still a good number of flowering stems left toward the end of the season.

• Start gathering seed as soon as the fruits and seedpods ripen; always clean, sort, and label all the gathered seed promptly to ensure it is not confused with other seed later on.

• Begin sowing seed in trays, cell packs, or in nursery beds to grow on under cover for a winter display.

• Make records of your successes and failures, personal preferences, and ideas for next year.

AUTUMN

• Continue sowing seed of annuals under cover for a display in late winter and early spring.

• Transplant first-year biennials from their nursery beds to their flowering positions in the open garden. Plant in groups for the most effective display.

STRAWFLOWER
SEEDHEAD

• Continue to gather seed as the fruits and seedheads ripen.

• Start to remove annual plants from containers as they finish flowering.

• Preserve any short-lived perennials used as bedding plants; plants such as geraniums and impatiens can be potted up and over-wintered in a frost-proof greenhouse or in the house. Alternatively, take stem-tip cuttings.

• Clean, dry, and package seeds for storing over winter, preferably in the refrigerator; remember to label them clearly.

• Order some seed catalogs to prepare for the following year's display.

CHOICE ANNUALS AND BIENNIALS

T HERE IS A VERY WIDE RANGE of annuals available to the gardener, both as
seed and as young plants. The majority are undemanding, given a well-
drained site that provides the appropriate light conditions. Plants are summer-
flowering unless otherwise stated.

☼ *Prefers full sun* ☀ *Prefers partial shade* ❈ *Dislikes transplanting* ◊ *Prefers well-drained
soil* ◑ *Prefers moist soil* **Small** *Up to 12in (30cm)* **Medium** *12–36in (30–90cm)*
Tall *Over 36in (90cm)* **Z** *Hardiness zone ranges (for biennials and short-lived perennials)
are given as Zx–x.*

A

Ageratum houstonianum
(Floss flower)
Mound-forming, small to
dwarf annual with oval leaves
and masses of pink, blue, or
white "powderpuff" flowers
in summer to autumn. Good
for butterflies. 'Blue Danube'
is dwarf, with sky blue
flowers; 'Bengali' has pale pink
flowers that darken with age.
Sow under cover in spring.
☼ ◊
'Adriatic' *p.36*

Agrostemma githago
(Corn cockle)
Elegant, medium annual with
paired, slender, pointed, gray-
green leaves and pink, trumpet-
blooms in summer. Good for
annual meadows and cutting.
Sow seed in spring.
☼ ❈ ◊
'Milas' *p.30*

AGROSTEMMA GITHAGO
'MILAS'

Alcea rosea (Hollyhock)
Tall biennials or short-lived
perennials, often grown as
annuals, with large, rough,
hand-shaped leaves and long
spikes of broad, funnel-
shaped, single or double
flowers in a wide range of
colors. 'Chater's Double'
grows to 8ft (2.5m) and bears

red, pink, yellow, or white
double flowers. 'Majorette'
is 2ft (60cm) and 'Summer
Carnival' is 6ft (2m), both
with flowers in many colors.
Sow under cover in late
summer or early spring.
☼ ◊ **Z3–9**

Amaranthus
Tall annuals with untoothed
foliage and dense, feathery,
or tassel-like clusters of tiny
flowers during summer.
A. hypochondriacus has erect,
broad, or flattened heads of
dark red flowers and purple-
flushed leaves. *A. caudatus*
(love-lies-bleeding) has hanging
flowerheads. *A. tricolor*
(Chinese spinach) is a bushy
annual grown for its leaves in
shades of red, purple, bronze,
and yellow, plus green. There
are several cultivars. Sow
outdoors in spring.
☼ ❈ ◊
A. caudatus p.37

◀ BRAZEN DAISIES *The brilliance of* Rudbeckia *'Radiant Gold' is softened by grasses in a border.*

Anchusa capensis (Alkanet)
Bushy, small to medium
biennial grown as an annual,
with bristly, lance-shaped
leaves and clusters of blue
forget-me-not-like flowers.
Good for attracting butterflies
and bees. The medium 'Blue
Bird' produces sky blue
flowers. Sow under cover in
summer or early spring.
☼ ◊
'Blue Angel' *p.30*

Anethum graveolens (Dill)
A popular, aromatic, medium,
annual herb (*p.22*) with finely
cut blue-green foliage and flat
heads of small, yellow-green
flowers. Good for cutting.
☼ ◊

Antirrhinum majus
(Snapdragon)
Small to medium perennial,
generally grown as an annual.
Bushy, with lance-shaped
leaves and spikes of fragrant,
pouched, two-lipped flowers
in a wide range of range of
colors as well as bicolors.
There are many selections,
from dwarf to tall, some with
open, bell-shaped flowers.

ANTIRRHINUM MAJUS
SONNET SERIES

ARCTOTIS FASTUOSA 'ZULU
PRINCE'

Sonnet Series is medium and
free-flowering. Sow under
cover in early spring or late
summer or outside in spring.
☼ ◊

Arctotis fastuosa (Monarch
of the veldt)
A medium annual with deeply
lobed, elliptical, silvery leaves
and large, orange daisies with
dark markings at the petal
bases and a blackish purple
disk, from midsummer until
autumn. 'Zulu Prince' has
white flowerheads and very
silver leaves. Harlequin
Hybrids (× *Venidioarctotis*)
have felty leaves and yellow,
orange, pink, white, apricot, or
red flowers. Good for cutting.
☼ ◊

Argemone (Prickly poppy)
Robust, medium, prickly
plants with thistlelike leaves.
Bears big, four-petaled poppy
flowers in summer, followed by
prickly seed pods. *A. mexicana*
has 3in (8cm) wide yellow or
orange flowers; *A. grandiflora*
(Z 8-11) has larger, white
flowers. Sow outside in spring.
☼ ❀ ◊

Atriplex hortensis
(Red mountain spinach,
Red orache)
Upright annual, to 4ft (1.2m),
with spinachlike foliage
in deep green to bronze or
purple-brown, or purple-red
in var. *rubra* (*p.6*). Bears long
clusters of tiny, reddish or
greenish brown flowers.
☼ ◊

B

Bassia scoparia f.
trichophylla, syn. *Kochia*
scoparia (Burning bush)
Medium, bushy, fast-growing
annual, grown for its feathery,
linear foliage, which turns
deep red in autumn. Sow
under cover in spring.
☼ ◊

Begonia semperflorens
Small, bushy, fleshy perennials
grown as annuals. The
rounded, fairly brittle leaves
are dark green, bronze,
reddish, or variegated. Plants
bear small clusters of single or
double flowers, in white, pink,
or red. Sow under cover in
early spring, or take stem
cuttings in summer and early
autumn.
☼ ◊
Begonia semperflorens *p.34,*
p.43. Also recommended:
Cocktail Series, 'Organdy'

Bellis perennis (English daisy)
A small, rosetted perennial
grown as a biennial, bearing
solitary, single, semi- or fully
double, button daisies above
the leaves on slender stalks.
Carpet Series and 'Goliath'
flowers are 3in (8cm) across,
'Pomponette' are 1in (2.5cm).
Both come in pink, red, white,

BORAGO OFFICINALIS

Bracteantha bracteata syn.
Helichrysum bracteata
(Golden everlasting,
Strawflower)
Small to medium, upright,
branching annual (*p.17, p.31*)
with lance-shaped leaves and
large, papery daisies in many
shades of red, yellow, orange,
pink, and white, with yellow
centers. Excellent for drying.
Good butterfly plant. Dwarf
to tall selections are available.
Sow seed in spring.
☼ ❁ ◊

Brassica oleracea
(Ornamental brassicas)
Cabbages and kales grown for
their colorful leaves; excellent
for autumn color. Osaka
Series make open, cabbagelike
plants to 18in (45cm), with
wavy, bluish green outer
leaves and pink or red centers.
'Tokyo' is similar but grows
to just 10in (25cm).
☼ ◊

Browallia speciosa
(Sapphire flower)
Medium, bushy perennial
grown as an annual, with oval
leaves and showy flowers in
violet-blue with white centers,
or white in the compact form
'White Troll'. Sow under
cover in early spring.
☼ ◊

C

Calendula officinalis
(Pot or English marigold)
Bushy annuals and short-lived
perennials with rough,
aromatic, succulent, elliptical,
pale green leaves and daisy-
like, single or double flowers
in yellow, orange, apricot, or
cream. Good for cutting.

CALLISTEPHUS CHINENSIS
'GIANT PRINCESS'

Many selections are available
in various sizes. Sow seed in
spring; often self-seeds.
☼ ◊

Callistephus chinensis
(China aster)
Medium or small, bushy
annuals with oval, toothed
leaves. Many selections, dwarf
and tall, with single, semi-,
or fully double, pompon or
quilled daisies, in a wide
range of colors. Tall types are
good for cutting. Sow every
few weeks to prolong bloom.
☼ ◊

Campanula medium
(Canterbury bells)
A medium biennial forming a
coarse, evergreen leaf-rosette
in the first year. Bears large
pyramids of bell-shaped, single
or double flowers in shades of
blue, purple, pink, or white in
late spring to early summer. In
'Cup and Saucer' the calyx,
normally green, is expanded,
saucerlike, and colored like
the petals. Sow under cover,
or in open ground in summer.
☼ ◊ **Z5–8**
C. isophylla 'Stella Blue' *p.4*

or bicolors. Sow under
cover in spring or outside
in summer.
☼ ◊ **Z4–8**

Bidens ferulifolia
Medium, spreading perennial
grown as an annual, with
finely cut foliage and bright
yellow daisies. Good for
containers. Sow under cover
in spring or take cuttings in
summer and early autumn.
☼ ◊

Borago officinalis (Borage)
Medium to tall, bristly annual,
sometimes overwintering, with
large, oval leaves and clusters
of nodding, star-shaped, blue
or white flowers. Excellent
bee flower. Sow seed in
spring; often self-seeds.
☼ ◊

Brachyscome iberidifolia
(Swan River daisy)
Small, spreading to trailing
annual (*p.42*) or short-lived
perennial with finely divided
green leaves and small blue,
pink, purple, or white daisies.
Sow in early spring.
☼ ◊

Capsicum annuum
(Chili pepper)
Small to medium, bushy
plants with lance-shaped to
elliptical, midgreen
(sometimes dark green,
purple, or variegated) leaves
and handsome, often
abundant, glossy round to
cone-shaped or fruits in
shades of yellow, orange,
purple, and red. A wide range
of cultivars is available. Sow
under cover in spring.
☼ ◐

Catharanthus roseus
(Madagascar periwinkle)
Medium, bushy perennial
grown as an annual with
glossy, dark green leaves and
showy white, pink, or red
flowers, many with a showy
"eye," from spring to frost.
Many cultivars are available.
Sow under cover in spring.
☼–☀ ◊

Celosia argentea
Small to medium, bushy
perennial grown as an annual,
with oval, mid-green leaves
and (in the Plumosa group)
pyramidal, feathery clusters of
tiny flowers in yellow, apricot,
pink, or red. In the Cristata
group, the flowers form a
flattened, often large and
monstrous, head resembling a
cock's comb. Sow under cover
in spring, or sow directly.
☼ ◊

Centaurea cyanus
(Cornflower)
A small to medium, upright
annual (p.33) with narrow,
lance-shaped, gray-green
leaves. Bears numerous blue,
purple, pink, or white daisy-
like flowers in summer. The
species is often used for

CLEOME HASSLERIANA
'ROSE QUEEN'

naturalizing; cultivars of
different heights are available.
Excellent for cutting. Sow in
autumn or early spring.
☼ ☼ ◊

Clarkia amoena syn.
Godetia amoena
An upright, medium annual
with lance-shaped leaves and
spikes of single or double
flowers with satiny, often
frilled petals in shades of
pink, mauve, and scarlet.
C. pulchella is taller, with
smaller flowers in a similar
color range. Sow in spring.
☼ ☼ ◊

Cleome hassleriana syn.
C. spinosa (Spider flower)
Tall, stout annual with hairy
stems and midgreen, handlike
leaves. Bears broad clusters of
strongly scented flowers with
narrow pink, mauve, purple,
or white petals and prominent
stamens. Cultivars have
showier flowers than the
species. Sow seed under cover
in spring, or sow directly.
☼ ◊
'Helen Campbell' p.15. Also
recommended: 'Rose Queen'

Consolida ajacis (Larkspur)
Tall, elegant annual with finely
cut, feathery foliage and large
spikes of single or double,
spurred flowers in blue, pink,
mauve, or white. Excellent for
cutting and for drying.
Cultivars in a range of heights
are available. Sow in spring,
or autumn in milder areas.
☼ ◐
Imperial Series p.37

Convolvulus tricolor
Upright to spreading annual
with funnel flowers in blue,
pink, or mauve, with white
and yellow centers, opening in
sun. Sow seed in spring.
☼ ◊
'Royal Ensign' p.31. Also
recommended: 'Blue Flash'

Coreopsis (Tickseed)
Medium, bushy plants with
green, lance-shaped leaves
and bright yellow daisies in
summer to early autumn.
C. tinctoria is an annual;
C. grandiflora, a perennial
(Z4-9) often grown as an
annual, has abundant yellow
flowers. Good for cutting.
☼ ◊

COREOPSIS TINCTORIA

RECOMMENDED CLIMBERS

Cardiospermum halicacabum (Balloon vine)
A fairly tall – to 10ft (3m) – tendriled, deciduous climber often grown as an annual. Slender stems bear attractive two-lobed leaves and inconspicuous flowers, followed in summer and autumn by inflated, lanternlike, straw-colored seed capsules. Sow seed under cover in spring.
☼ ◐

Cobaea scandens
(Cup and saucer vine)
Rampant, tendriled climber with deep green leaves and solitary, bell-shaped flowers that are green when they open and age to purple, or to white in f. *alba*. Sow under cover in spring.
☼ ◑

Eccremocarpus scaber
(Chilean glory vine)
Tendriled evergreen, to 12ft (4m), grown as an annual but often overwintering. Has dissected, gray-green leaves and long-stalked clusters of tubular flowers in red, orange or pink, followed by pendent, lemon-shaped, inflated seed pods.
☼ ◑

Ipomoea (Morning glory)
Twining climbers with heart-shaped leaves and funnel-shaped flowers. *I. alba* (Moonflower), grows to 22ft (7m), with large (6in/15cm), fragrant white flowers that open at dusk. Grows well in

LABLAB PURPUREUS

a large container. The morning glory, *I. tricolor*, to 12ft (4m), has white, blue, purple, or reddish flowers that usually fade by the afternoon.
☼ ◐
'Grandpa Ott' *p.15*, **I. lobata** *p.25*, **I.** *tricolor* 'Heavenly Blue' *p.33*

Lablab purpureus
(Hyacinth bean)
Vigorous, twining, deciduous perennial grown as an annual, to 15ft (5m), with three-part leaves and purple pea flowers followed by showy, purple-red, shiny seedpods. Sow seed under cover in spring.
☼ ◐

Lathyrus odoratus
(Sweet pea)
Annual (*p.24*) with winged stems to 10ft (3m). Bears long-stalked clusters of large, finely scented pea flowers in many colors except yellow. Many cultivars are available, mostly climbing. Ideal cut flower. Sow under cover in autumn or early spring.
☼ ◑

Rhodochiton atrosanguineus
Twining perennial grown as an annual (*p.25*) to 10ft (3m), with heart-shaped leaves. Drooping, tubular, reddish purple flowers in summer and autumn have hatlike, pinkish calyces.
☼ ◑

Thunbergia alata (Black-eyed Susan vine)
Twining annual (*p.40*) to 10ft (3m), with arrowhead-shaped leaves and showy, sideways-facing, trumpet flowers in orange, cream, yellow, or apricot, all with black centers. Sow seed under cover in spring.
☼ ◐

Tropaeolum
T. majus (nasturtium) climbs to 10ft (3m), with spurred flowers mainly in red, orange, yellow, and pink.
T. peregrinum, to 8ft (2.5m), has yellow, birdlike flowers. Sow under cover in early spring, outside in late spring.
☼ ◐
T. peregrinum p.25

LATHYRUS ODORATUS 'MARS'

Cosmos bipinnatus
(Cosmos)
A branched annual to 5ft
(1.5m) with feathery foliage
and large, daisylike flowers in
pink, mauve, red, and white.
Good for cutting. Modern
selections are often only 2ft
(60cm) tall. *C. sulphureus* has
golden flowers. Sow in spring.
☼ ◊

D

Dahlia
The smaller perennial bedding
or border dahlias grown as
annuals are bushy, 8–20in
(20–50cm) tall, with deep
green, fleshy leaves and
numerous single, semi-, or
fully double flowers in many
shades except blue. Good for
cutting. Many selections are
available. Sow under cover in
spring; take cuttings or divide
in spring.
☼ ◊
Recommended: 'Redskin',
Unwin's Dwarf Group

Dianthus (Pink)
Small to medium, bushy plants
with lance-shaped to linear

Dahlia Coltness hybrid

Dianthus 'Cherry Picotee'

leaves and fragrant, usually
fringed flowers, mostly in red,
pink, and white, often finely
marked. Good for cutting.
D. barbatus (sweet William, Z
3-9) has dense, flat flowerheads.
D. chinensis (Chinese or
Indian pink) has fringed,
single or double blooms. Sow
in spring or early summer.
☼ ◊
D. 'Telstar' p.17

Digitalis (Foxglove)
Softly downy biennial or
short-lived perennial, forming
a coarse, evergreen leaf rosette
in the first year. Flowers are
tubular, purple, pink, yellow,
or white, often spotted
within, in dense, one-sided,
tapered spikes up to 4ft
(1.2m). Excellent for bees and
naturalizing. Sow in spring or
summer; often self-seeds.
☼ ◊ **Z4–8**
D. purpurea p.32, p.53

Dimorphotheca pluvialis
(Rain daisy)
Small, bushy annual (*p.30*)
with dark green, elliptical
leaves and large white daisies
with brownish purple centers,
opening in sun. Sow in spring.
☼ ◊

Dorotheanthus bellidiformis
(Livingstone daisy,
Mesembryanthemum)
Low, carpeting annual with
gray, "crystalline" leaves and
daisies in vivid shades of
yellow, red, pink, or white,
often with dark centers,
opening in sun. Sow seed in
early spring under cover.
☼ ◊

E

Echium vulgare
(Viper's bugloss)
Small to medium, bushy, bristly
annual or biennial with lance-
shaped leaves and spiraled
clusters of tubular flowers in
shades of purple, pink, blue,
or white. Dwarf forms are
available. Sow in spring.
☼ ◊ **Z3–8**

Eryngium giganteum
(Miss Willmott's ghost)
Tall biennial with very prickly
leaves and thistlelike, blue
flowerheads and prominent,
hollylike, silvery bracts.
Excellent for drying. Sow in
spring; often self-seeds. (In the
first year, rosette is not spiny.)
☼ ◊ **Z5–8**

Erysimum cheiri
syn. *Cheiranthus cheiri*
(Wallflower)
A medium, bushy biennial or
short-lived perennial with deep
green, elliptical leaves and
clusters of sweetly scented
flowers in red, yellow, orange,
bronze, and cream in spring.
Good for bedding with bulbs.
Many selections available,
including dwarf types. Sow
seed in early summer.
☼ ◊ **Z3–7**
'Fire King' *p.14*

Euphorbia marginata

Eschscholzia californica
(California poppy)
Small to medium, rather succulent annual (*p.31*), sometimes overwintering, with gray- or blue-green, fern-

like foliage. The four-petaled, satiny flowers come in shades of yellow, orange, red, pink, and apricot, sometimes bicolored, and open in sun. The many selections include types with frilled and semi-double flowers. Sow in spring, or in autumn in mild areas.
☼ ◊
E. lobbii p.32, 'Yellow Cap' *p.14*

Euphorbia marginata
(Snow-on-the-mountain)
An upright, medium, bushy annual with elliptical, bright green leaves. The numerous attractive bracts surround insignificant greenish flowers. Sow seed in spring. Reseeds.
☼ ◊

Exacum affine (Persian violet)
Small, bushy annual (*p.42*) with bright green, succulent, oval leaves. Bears numerous small flowers in blue, violet, or purple in late spring and summer. Good for containers. Sow in late summer or spring.
☼ ◑

F

Felicia amelloides
(Blue daisy)
Small, bushy shrub grown as an annual, with oval leaves and yellow-centered, blue daisies. Sow seed under cover in early spring or take stem cuttings in summer.
☼ ◑

RECOMMENDED GRASSES

Briza maxima (Greater quaking grass)
An upright, slender, medium annual (*p.23*, *p.56*) with mid-green leaves, mainly at the base, and sprays of nodding purplish green flowers. Very good for drying. Sow in spring; self-seeds readily.
☼ ◊

Hordeum jubatum
(Foxtail barley)
Medium, tufted annual or short-lived perennial (*p.23*). The feathery, arched plumes are flushed pink, then straw-colored. Sow in spring.
☼ ◊ **Z4–8**

Lagurus ovatus (Hare's-tail grass)
Small to medium, tufted annual with pale green leaves and pointed, soft

white flowerheads with yellow stamens. Good for drying. Sow seed in spring.
☼ ◊

Pennisetum setaceum
(Fountain grass)
A tall, tufted, perennial grass that is often grown as an annual, with rough, mid-green leaves and cylindrical

Lagurus ovatus

spikes of copper-red that last well into winter. Sow seed in spring.
☼ ◊

Setaria italica
(Foxtail millet)
Tall, tufted annual grass with narrow, lance-shaped leaves and lax heads of white, cream, yellow, red, brown, or black. Good for drying. Sow in late spring.
☼ ☼ ◊

Zea mays (Corn, Maize)
Medium to tall annual; the female flowers develop into the ears. Some cultivars ("Indian corn") have multicolored ears that dry extremely well; others have variegated leaves. Sow in late spring.
☼ ◑

G

Gaillardia pulchella
(Blanket flower)
Medium, upright, bushy annual with gray-green, lance-shaped leaves and single to fully double daisies in yellow, red, pink, or crimson, often bicolored. Good for cutting. Sow seed in spring.

☼ ◊

Gazania
Low-growing perennials, often grown as annuals, with lance-shaped, leathery, deep green to white-felted leaves and large daisies, often in bright yellow, orange, or red with darker central markings, sometimes cream, white, or pink. Sow seed in early spring.

☼ ◊
Daybreak Series *p.41.*
Also recommended: Talent Series, Chansonette Series.

Gilia
Medium annuals with feathery foliage and button flowerheads from summer to early autumn. *G. capitata* (Queen Anne's thimbles) has lavender-blue flowers. *G. tricolor* (bird's-eyes) has violet flowers with orange or yellow centers and purple spots. Sow in spring.

☼ ◊

Glaucium corniculatum
(Red horned poppy)
Medium biennial or short-lived perennial with oblong, lobed, silvery gray leaves and orange, bowl-shaped flowers followed by long, curved seedpods. Similar, but with bluish leaves and dark orange to crimson flowers, is *G. grandiflorum*.

☼ ◊ **Z6–9**

Gomphrena globosa
(Globe amaranth)
Small, bushy annual with oval, hairy leaves and pink, purple, orange, yellow, or white, cloverlike flowerheads. Good for cutting. Sow under cover or in open ground in spring.

☼ ◊

Gypsophila elegans
(Annual baby's breath)
A medium, upright, branched annual (*p.5*) with gray-green, lance-shaped leaves and spreading sprays of numerous small, white flowers. Excellent for cutting. Sow in spring.

☼ ☼ ◊

H

Helianthus annuus
(Sunflower)
A rough, hairy annual to 10ft (3m), with 1 erect stem, ace-of-spade leaves, and 8–16in (20–40cm) flowerheads with brown or purple disks (*p.56*). Some have double flowers, others smaller flowers and branched stems; dwarf forms are 12–20in (30–50cm) tall. Flowers range from cream, orange, and yellow to brown and rust. Good for cutting and drying. Sow in spring.

☼ ◊
H. 'Pastiche' p.22

HELIANTHUS 'GIANT SINGLE'

HELIOTROPIUM ARBORESCENS

Helichrysum petiolare
Medium, spreading to trailing, evergreen shrub grown as an annual. The small, silver-gray, round to heart-shaped leaves are very attractive; the sparse flowers are creamy yellow. Take semi-ripe cuttings in summer.

☼ ◊
'Variegatum' *p.19*

Heliophila coronopifolia
Low-growing to medium, rather slender annual with simple or lobed leaves and numerous small, blue, four-petaled flowers with yellow-green centers. Sow in spring.

☼ ☼ ◊

Heliotropium arborescens
(Heliotrope, Cherry pie)
Bushy, evergreen shrub grown as an annual, with glossy, deep green, narrow, wrinkled leaves and dense, flat clusters of sweetly scented, lavender to purple flowers. Cultivars come in blue, purple, pink, and white. Sow seed in spring, or take cuttings in summer and early autumn.

☼ ◊

Hibiscus

Annuals or short-lived perennials with lobed leaves and funnel-shaped flowers that open in sun. *H. acetosella* 'Coppertone' has striking maroon-purple leaves. *H. trionum* (flower-of-an-hour) is medium height with creamy yellow flowers with purple-brown centers. Sow under cover in early spring; take cuttings in summer.

☼ ◊

Hunnemannia fumariifolia

(Mexican tulip poppy) Short-lived perennial grown as an annual, with large, bright yellow flowers. It looks like *Eschscholzia* (*see p.67*) but has coarser leaves. Good for cutting. Sow in spring.

☼ ❀ ◊

I

Iberis umbellata (Candytuft)

Mound-forming annual with lance-shaped leaves and flat heads of pink, purple, or white flowers in summer to early autumn. Sow in spring, or in autumn in mild areas.

☼ ❀ ◊

Impatiens (Balsam)

Succulent, small to medium annuals or perennials grown as annuals, with lance-shaped to elliptical, serrated leaves. The common impatiens (*I. walleriana*) is spreading, with spurred, flat flowers in hues of apricot, purple, pink, red, orange, and white. Good for containers and bedding; tolerates shade. *I. balsamina* (Rose balsam) is upright, with narrow, lance-shaped leaves and hooded, single or double,

IMPATIENS NEW GUINEA GROUP

pink, red, purple, mauve, or white flowers borne on the main stem. New Guinea Group are bushy and upright with large leaves, often marked with bronze, red, or yellow, and large, flat, spurred blooms in purple, pink, white, scarlet, or orange Seedpods explode when ripe to expel the seed. Sow seed in early spring under cover or take cuttings in summer.

☼ ◑ ◊

Mixed hybrids *p.5, p.34, p.45,* **Super Elfin Series** *p.41,* **Tempo Series** *p.43*

L

Lantana camara

Scrambling, evergreen shrub, usually grown as an annual, with finely wrinkled, oval leaves and rounded heads of small, orange, yellow, purple, pink, red, and white flowers all summer. Flowers often open pale and darken to a different shade; those in the center open last. Similar *L. montevidensis* has violet or white flowers.

☼ ◊

Lavatera trimestris

Vigorous, tall, leafy annual (*p.33*) with heart-shaped, lobed leaves and large, satiny, funnel-shaped flowers in summer and early autumn. 'Silver Cup' has rose-pink flowers with deeper veins; 'Mont Blanc' has white flowers. Sow seed in spring.

☼ ◊

'Mont Blanc' *p.31*

Layia platyglossa

(Tidy tips) Fast-growing, small to medium annual with gray-green, lance-shaped leaves and abundant, small, daisy-like flowers in yellow, ringed with white. Excellent for butterflies and for cutting. Sow seed in early spring.

☼ ◊

Leucanthemum paludosum

A small, bushy annual (*p.35*) with oval to wedge-shaped, lobed or toothed leaves and small, solitary, yellow daisies with a darker center. 'Show Star' has yellow-green foliage. Sow seed in spring.

☼ ◊

LEUCANTHEMUM PALUDOSUM 'SHOW STAR'

Limnanthes douglasii
(Poached-egg plant)
Small, spreading annual with bright green, pinnate leaves (*p.27*). It has egg-yolk yellow, saucer-shaped flowers, usually ringed with white, in late spring to early summer. Sow in autumn or spring; self-seeds.
☼ ◐

Limonium sinuatum (Sea lavender, Statice)
Medium, erect perennial grown as an annual (*p.20*), with a basal rosette of dull green, wavy-edged, oblong leaves, and branched spikes of everlasting, papery flowers in pink, red, purple, mauve, yellow, and white. Excellent for drying; good for butterflies.
☼ ◊

Linaria maroccana
Small, bushy annual with pale green, linear to lance-shaped leaves and slender clusters of small, two-lipped flowers in pink, red, purple, yellow, white, or bicolors, with a pointed spur. Sow in spring.
☼ ◊

Linum grandiflorum
'Rubrum' (Flax)
Upright, small to medium annual with lance-shaped leaves and vivid saucer-shaped flowers (*p.32*). Sow in spring.
☼ ❀ ◊

Lobelia erinus
Tufted or trailing annuals, sometimes overwintering, with oval to lance-shaped, green to bronze or purple leaves and many small, two-lipped flowers in blue, pink, purple, red, mauve, or white. Excellent for bedding; trailing types are also good for containers. Sow

under cover in early spring.
☼ ◐
'Cambridge Blue' *p.36*,
'Crystal Palace' *p.32*,
'Sapphire' *p.40*,
'Snowball' *p.32*

Lobularia maritima
(Sweet alyssum)
Small, tufted to mat-forming annual with narrow, lance-shaped, gray-green leaves and dense clusters of tiny, sweetly scented flowers in pink, purple, or white as in 'Snowflake'. Excellent for edging. Many cultivars available. Good butterfly plant. Sow in spring.
☼ ◊
L. **Easter Bonnet Series** *p.26*

Lunaria annua (Honesty)
Biennial growing to 30in (75cm), forming a lax rosette of heart-shaped leaves in the first year; produces branched clusters of purple, scented, four-petaled flowers in spring and early summer, then flat, silvery seedpods (*p.21, p.56*) that are excellent for drying. 'Variegata' has paler flowers and cream-variegated leaves.
☼ ◊ **Z5–9**

LOBULARIA MARITIMA
'LITTLE DORRIT'

Lupinus (Lupine)
Annual lupines are medium to tall, with rounded, deeply divided leaves and small, pea-like flowers borne in dense, tapering spikes. *L. hartwegii* blooms are pale blue, *L. luteus* bright yellow. Sow in spring.
☼ ❀ ◊

M

Malcolmia maritima
(Virginia stock)
Small, fast-growing annual with gray-green leaves and sparse clusters of dainty, scented flowers in red, pink, or white, spring and summer. Sow in succession in spring and early summer, or autumn.
☼ ◊

Malope trifida
(Annual mallow)
Tall annual with lobed leaves and large, satiny, funnel-shaped flowers in purple-red with deeper veins. 'Vulcan' has bright magenta-pink flowers. Sow seed in spring.
☼ ◊

MALOPE TRIFIDA
'VULCAN'

MATTHIOLA INCANA
CINDERELLA SERIES

MENTZELIA LINDLEYI

Matthiola incana
(Stock)
A medium, bushy biennial or short-lived perennial (p.26), with elliptical, gray leaves and sweetly scented, four-petaled flowers. 'Giant Excelsior' is tall, with pink, red, pale-blue, or white double flowers. The shorter Cinderella Series also has dark blues. Ten Week Series is fast-growing, with single flowers in many shades. Sow under cover in spring.
☼ ◑ Z7–8

Meconopsis betonicifolia
(Himalayan poppy)
Tall biennial or perennial with bristly leaves and large, open poppylike flowers in violet, blue, or mauve, with yellow anthers. Needs acidic soil.
☀ ◑ Z7–8

Mentzelia lindleyi
syn. *Bartonia aurea*
(Blazing star)
Fast growing, medium, bushy annual with fernlike leaves and bright yellow flowers with pointed petals. Good for cutting. Sow in spring.
☼ ✳ ◊

Mimulus (Monkey flower)
Succulent, spreading annuals or short-lived perennials with fresh green, toothed, elliptical foliage. The flowers, like open snapdragons, are often spotted or blotched. *M. guttatus* has bright yellow flowers with reddish brown blotches. Sow seed under cover in spring.
☼ ◐
M. Malibu Series *p.41*

Mirabilis jalapa
(Marvel of Peru, Four o'clock)
Medium, bushy perennial, usually grown as an annual or biennial, with oval, midgreen leaves and long, trumpet-shaped flowers in magenta, red, pink, yellow, or white, often with several colors on the same flower, opening late in the afternoon.
☀ ◐

Moluccella laevis
(Bells of Ireland)
Medium, erect annual (p.14) with round, pale green leaves and small, white flowers, each backed by a conspicuous, green, persistent, collarlike

calyx. Excellent for cutting and drying. Sow under cover or outdoors in late spring.
☼ ◊

Myosotis sylvatica
(Forget-me-not)
Small, tufted annual or biennial with elliptical, gray-green leaves and spirals of small blue flowers in spring and summer. Many cultivars include ones with blue, violet, pink, or white flowers, and compact types for formal bedding. 'Music' is erect, with large, bright blue flowers. Sow in spring or summer.
☼ ◊ Z5–9

N

Nemesia strumosa
Small, bushy annual with lance-shaped, serrated leaves and two-lipped, funnel-shaped flowers in a range of bright colors. The compact forms such as Triumph Series are excellent for formal bedding.
☼ ◊
'Fragrant Cloud *p.19*,
N. versicolor **'Blue Bird'** *p.14*

MYOSOTIS SYLVATICA
'MUSIC'

Nemophila menziesii
(Baby blue-eyes)
Small, delicate annual with
narrow, serrated, gray-green
leaves and small, saucer-
shaped, bright blue flowers
with white centers.
☼ ◊
N. maculata p.19

Nicotiana (Flowering tobacco)
Medium annual with
elliptical, sticky leaves and lax
clusters of long-throated, flat-
faced flowers in summer and
autumn. *N. alata* has white
flowers, brownish violet on
the outside, opening and
strongly scented at evening.
N. × sanderae hybrids are
popular for bedding and for
containers, in shades of green,
red, pink, purple, and white,
the latter often scented. Sow
seed under cover in spring.
☼ ◊
N. 'Lime Green' p.40. Also
recommended: *N. langsdorfii* ♥

Nierembergia caerulea
syn. *N. hippomanica*
Small, bushy perennial grown
as an annual with lance-
shaped leaves and

bowl-shaped, five-lobed, blue,
violet, or purple flowers – or
white in 'Mont Blanc' – in
summer and early autumn.
Sow under cover in spring.
☼ ◊
Also recommended: 'Purple
Robe'

Nigella damascena
(Love-in-a-mist)
Medium, upright annual with
flat, multipetalled flowers
backed by a ruff of feathery
leaves and followed by
inflated seed capsules (*p.2*),
excellent for drying. Persian
Jewels Series has blue, pink,
or white flowers; 'Miss Jekyll'
has rich blue flowers.
N. hispanica has unruffled
purple flowers and dark seed
capsules. Sow seed in autumn
or spring; often self-seeds.
☼ ☼ ◊
Persian Jewels Series *p.31*

O

Ocimum basilicum (Basil)
A small to medium, highly
aromatic culinary herb with
elliptical, shiny, deep green

foliage and spikes of small,
two-lipped flowers in pink or
white. Many cultivars are
available, including some with
leaves in bronzy purple, as in
'Dark Opal', or with ruffled
edges. Sow seed successively
from late spring.
☼ ◊

Oenothera biennis
(Evening primrose)
A tall, stiff-stemmed biennial
with elliptical, gray-green
leaves and primrose yellow,
scented cuplike flowers that
unfurl in the evening. Sow in
spring; often self-seeds.
☼ ◊ **Z4–8**

Onopordum acanthium
(Scotch thistle)
An imposing, tall, extremely
prickly biennial, forming a
large, spiny-leaved rosette in
the first year, then growing to
6ft (1.8m). The stem is very
leafy, with spiny wings, and
branched above to carry
the relatively large, purple,
typical thistle flowerheads.
Good for drying. Sow seed in
spring or summer.
☼ ◊ **Z6–9**

NIEREMBERGIA CAERULEA
'MONT BLANC'

OCIMUM BASILICUM
'DARK OPAL'

OSTEOSPERMUM
'WHIRLIGIG'

PAPAVER SOMNIFERUM   *PELARGONIUM* HORIZON SERIES   *PETUNIA* CARPET SERIES

Osteospermum
Short to medium perennials, often grown as annuals, with oval to elliptical leaves and showy daisies in white, yellow, purple, or pink, often with a contrasting central disk, in summer and autumn. Species include *O. ecklonis* (white with a dark blue disk), *O. fruticosum* (white with a purplish violet disk), and *O. jucundum* (mauve-pink to magenta with a purple disk). Some cultivars have crimped petals. Sow seed in spring.
☼ ◊

P

Papaver (Poppy)
Genus with lobed or divided leaves and showy, four-petaled flowers. *P. croceum* (Iceland poppy, Z 2-8) is a small perennial usually grown as a biennial with blue-green foliage and large flowers in pink, white, yellow, orange, or red. *P. rhoeas* (corn poppy) has deep green leaves and red flowers with black centers. *P. commutatum* has scarlet flowers with a large black

blotch in the center of each petal. *P. somniferum* (opium poppy) is taller, to 3ft (90cm), with fleshy, waxy, gray-green leaves, large flowers in pink, mauve, red, purple, and almost black, and decorative seedpods. Double-flowered forms are widely available, with their petals fringed ('Carnation Flowered') or entire ('Peony Flowered'). Sow in spring; often self-seeds.
☼ ◊
P. somniferum p.21, p.44,
P. rhoeas. **Shirley Series** *p.31*

Pelargonium
Popular perennials grown as annuals for containers and bedding, with aromatic leaves and long-stalked clusters of flowers in red, pink, purple, orange, and white. Zonal types have rounded leaves marked with a darker band and large heads of single or double flowers. Ivy-leaved types are trailing or climbing with lobed, fairly fleshy leaves and more spidery flowers. Unique types, like 'Voodoo', are shrubby, with pungent leaves and single flowers.
☼ ◊

Multibloom Pink *p.36, p.41.*
Also recommended: Orbit Series, Diamond Series

Penstemon
Medium to tall, short-lived perennials often grown as annuals. Usually bushy, with lance-shaped leaves and long, one-sided spikes of tubular to bell-shaped flowers in purple, red, pink, mauve, or white. Cutting-grown cultivars and seed selections are available. Sow under cover in spring or autumn, or take softwood cuttings in summer.
☼ ◊

Petunia
Bushy, often sticky, short-lived perennials grown as annuals, with oval to elliptical, matte green leaves and single, frilled, or double, funnel-shaped flowers, some finely scented, in diverse hues. Smaller, bushy types, such as Carpet Series, are excellent for bedding; trailing ones, such as weather-resistant Surfinia Series, are ideal for containers. Sow under cover in early spring.
☼ ◊
Surfinia Series *p.43*

PHLOX DRUMMONDII
'PALONA LIGHT SALMON'

Phacelia campanularia
(California bluebell)
Compact, bushy annual with oval, deep green leaves and numerous small, bell-shaped, deep blue flowers. Excellent for attracting bees and butterflies. Sow in spring.
☼ ✳ ◊

Phlox drummondii
(Annual phlox)
Small, bushy annual with lance-shaped, pale green leaves. Flowers are borne in dense clusters and may be flat-faced and long-throated (as in the Palona Series) or star-shaped, both in a range of pastel or bright colors, often patterned, bicolored, or zoned. Good for bedding. Sow under cover in spring.
☼ ◊
'Sternenzauber' *p.10*

Portulaca grandiflora
(Rose moss, Sun plant)
A low-growing, spreading, fleshy annual with red stems and narrow, pointed, bright green leaves. Bears fairly large, satiny, bowl-shaped, single or double flowers in bright shades of yellow, orange, red, pink, or white. Sow in spring.
☼ ◊

Psylliostachys suworowii
(Statice)
A medium, erect, fairly slow-growing annual with lobed, lance-shaped leaves and erect, slender, pipe-cleaner spikes of tiny, bright pink flowers, good for drying. Sow in spring under cover, late spring in the open.
☼ ◊

R

Reseda odorata
(Mignonette)
Medium, pale green, erect to spreading annual with narrow, oval leaves, and fat spikes of small, greenish white, powerfully scented flowers. Sow seed in spring.
☼ ✳ ◊

Ricinus communis
(Castor bean)
An imposing evergreen shrub, usually grown as an annual foliage accent(*p.36*).

RESEDA ODORATA

RUDBECKIA HIRTA
'RUSTIC DWARFS'

The leaves are very large, handlike, and often deep bronze or purplish. Short spikes of small, red flowers precede prickly seedpods.
☼ ◊

Rudbeckia hirta
Medium biennial or short-lived perennial (*p.30*), often grown as an annual, with rough, lance-shaped, midgreen leaves and large, yellow daisies with conical brown centers. Good for cutting. 'Marmalade' has golden flowers with black cones. Sow seed in spring.
☼ ◊ Z3–7
'Radiant Gold' *p.60*

S

Salpiglossis sinuata
Medium, upright, lanky annuals with lance-shaped, sticky, light green leaves. Trumpet flowers occur in bright shades of yellow, orange, red, and blue and are conspicuously veined. Sow under cover in early spring.
☼ ◊

SALVIA SPLENDENS
'SCARLET KING'

Salvia (Sage)

Square-stemmed annuals or perennials grown as annuals, with whorled spikes of showy, two-lipped flowers. *S. farinacea* is tall, with lance-shaped leaves and white, blue, or violet flower spikes. *S. patens* is medium, with lax spikes of large, deep blue flowers. *S. coccinea* is tall, with oval, serrated leaves and red flowers. *S. splendens* is low to medium and bushy with oval, serrated, fresh green leaves and dense scarlet flowers and bracts. Cultivars in violet, purple, pink, white, salmon, or red (as in 'Scarlet King') all make excellent bedding. *S. viridis* (annual clary) is medium with pink or pale flowers tipped by bracts in blue, purple, pink, or white. Sow under cover in spring; sow *S. viridis* in open ground.
☼ ◊

S. splendens Cleopatra Series *p.36, S. viridis p.27*

Sanvitalia procumbens

(Creeping zinnia)
A mat-forming, prostrate annual with oval, pointed, bright green leaves and many small, yellow daisies with black centers. Sow in spring.
☼ ◊

Scabiosa (Pincushion flower, Scabious)

Bushy annuals with flat flowerheads, the outer florets being the largest. Biennials and short-lived perennials are usually grown as annuals. *S. atropurpurea* (sweet scabious) is tall with lance-shaped leaves and purple, blue, white, or crimson flowers. *S. stellata* (starry scabious) is medium with lyre-shaped leaves and pale flowers and decorative, beige, starry seedheads, good for drying. Sow in spring.
☼ ◊

Scaevola aemula

Low to medium, spreading to trailing perennial grown as an annual, with lance-shaped to oval leaves and clusters of blue, lilac, violet, or white, lobelia-like flowers. Excellent for containers. Sow seed under cover in spring.
☼ ◊
'New Wonder' *p.40*

Schizanthus pinnatus

(Poor man's orchid)
Bushy annuals with feathery green leaves and large clusters of showy, orchidlike flowers in varied hues with contrasting markings, often with a yellow or white center. Excellent in containers. Sow seed in spring, or in late summer for flowering under cover.
☼ ◊

Senecio cineraria

A medium, mound-forming, evergreen shrub, usually

SENECIO CINERARIA
'SILVER DUST'

grown as an annual, with handsome, variously lobed, silver-gray foliage (*p.34*). Bears clusters of mustard yellow flowerheads on long stalks in the second summer.
☼ ◊

Silene armeria

(Sweet William catchfly)
A small to medium, upright annual or biennial, with paired, oval, gray-green leaves and branched clusters of rose-pink, star-shaped flowers, with slightly notched petals, in summer and early autumn. Good for butterflies. Sow in spring or summer.
☼ ◊

Silybum marianum

(Mary's thistle)
A tall, coarse biennial that forms a large, flat leaf-rosette in the first year. The leaves are quite broad, deeply lobed, glossy, spiny, and deep green in color with bold white or silver marbling. The purple, thistlelike flowers should be removed for the best foliage. Sow seed in spring.
☼ ◊ **Z6–9**

Smyrnium perfoliatum
Medium to tall, erect biennial.
The upper leaves and bracts
are oval, bright yellow-green,
and encircle the stem. Bears
small heads of tiny, greenish
yellow flowers. Sow in early
spring; often self-seeds.
☼ ◊ Z6–9

Solanum pseudocapsicum
(Christmas cherry, Jerusalem
cherry, Winter cherry)
Evergreen, bushy perennial,
grown as an annual, with
lance-shaped leaves. Small,
starry, white flowers precede
showy, round, scarlet fruits.
Sow under cover in spring.
☼ ◊

Solenostemon scutellarioides
(Coleus)
A bushy, evergreen perennial
grown as an annual. "Ace-of-
spade" leaves are marked in
shades of pink, yellow, green,
red, or purpleand are usually
multicolored. Remove flower
spikes to encourage new
shoots and promote bushiness.
Sow under cover in spring;
take cuttings anytime.
☼ ◊
Wizard Series *p.16*

Sutera grandiflora
Small to medium, spreading
perennial grown as an annual
with small, oval leaves and
pink, white, or purple, frilled,
long-throated, flat-faced
flowers in summer and
autumn. Good container
plant. Sow under cover in
early spring or take softwood
cuttings in summer.
☼ ◊
'Knysna Hills' *p.42*, **'Sea
Mist'** *p.40*

T

Tagetes (Marigold)
Strongly aromatic, stiff, bushy
annuals with finely divided
foliage and many daisy- or
carnation-like flowers. French
marigold cultivars, bred from
T. patula, have single to fully
double flowers in yellow,
orange, mahogany, or red, or
bicolored or zoned. Popular
for bedding and containers.
Many varieties are available
from tall to dwarf. African
marigold cultivars come from
T. erecta, a medium to tall
plant with large, single to
fully double flowers in gold,

cream, or orange. Small-
flowered Signet marigolds are
bred from *T. tenuifolia*. Sow
under cover in spring.
☼ ◊
'Golden Gem' *p.36*

Tanacetum parthenium
(Feverfew)
A medium, bushy biennial or
short-lived perennial (*p.18*).
The aromatic, deeply lobed,
oblong leaves are midgreen,
but golden-green in 'Aureum'.
Bears broad clusters of small,
white daisies with gold centers.
Sow in spring; often self-seeds.
☼ ◊ Z4–9

Thymophylla tenuiloba
(Dahlberg daisy)
A medium, much-branched
annual with fernlike leaves
and small, orange-yellow
daisies in late spring and
summer. Sow seed in spring.
☼ ◊

Tithonia rotundifolia
syn. *T. speciosa* (Mexican
sunflower)
Tall, upright annual with
triangular to oval, often lobed
leaves, and 3in (8cm) bright
orange or scarlet, zinnia-like

SMYRNIUM PERFOLIATUM

TAGETES 'TANGERINE GEM'

THYMOPHYLLA TENUILOBA

flowerheads. Good for cutting. Sow under cover in spring.

☼ ◊

Torenia fournieri
(Wishbone flower)
Small, bushy annual (*p.42*) with serrated, elliptical, fairly pale leaves and flared, tubular, two-lipped flowers of pale blue-purple, with purple-black bases. Good container plant. Sow under cover in spring.

☼ ◊
'Blue Moon' *p.16*

Trachelium caeruleum
syn. *Diosphaera caeruleum* (Blue throatwort)
Tall perennial grown as an annual, with oval, serrated leaves and dense clusters of small lilac flowers. Good for butterflies and cutting. Sow under cover in early spring.

☼ ◊

Tropaeolum majus
(Nasturtium)
Dwarf nasturtiums (*see also p.65*) form medium, bushy plants. The flowers are edible. Sow seed in spring, but take stem-tip cuttings of named forms like 'Hermine Grashoff'.

☼ ◊
Alaska Series p.7, 'Hermine Grashoff' *p.40*

V

Verbascum olympicum
(Mullein)
Handsome, tall biennial that forms a large, gray-felted rosette in the first year; in the second, many small, bright yellow flowers are borne in branching spires on felted stems. *V. bombyciferum* is even larger, to 6ft (2m), with

VERBENA 'IMAGINATION'

silver-white foliage. Sow in spring; sometimes self-seeds.

☼ ◊ Z5–9

Verbena
Verbena bonariensis is a tall biennial (Z 7-11) with sparse, oblong leaves and small, red-purple flowerheads that attract butterflies. Hybrid verbenas, good in containers, are spreading, trailing perennials grown as annuals. They have narrow, toothed foliage and dense, flat heads of small flowers in vivid pink, blue, mauve, white, and red, often with yellow or white eyes. Sow under cover in spring.

☼ ◊
'Imagination' *p.41*, 'Tapien Pink' *p.43*

Viola (Pansy)
Low-growing annual or short-lived perennial with toothed, oval leaves and flowers in varied sizes, hues, bicolors, or patterned "faces." Ideal for formal and informal bedding. Sow under cover or outdoors in late winter.

☼ ◊
'Romeo and Juliet' *p.15*, 'Sorbet Yellow Frost' *p.39*

X

Xeranthemum annuum
(Immortelle)
A tufted, medium annual with lance-shaped, silver leaves and purple daisies with silver, papery, "everlasting" bracts. Dries well. Sow in spring.

☼ ◊

Z

Zinnia
Zinnia elegans is an upright to bushy annual with rough, oval to lance-shaped leaves and showy flowers mainly in pink, red, purple, yellow, and cream. There are cultivars in all sizes, with single, double, or pompon flowerheads; 'Envy' needs a bit of shade. Good for cutting.
Z. haageana (Mexican zinnia) is a medium annual with narrow, lance-shaped leaves. Sow under cover in spring or outdoors late spring.

☼ ◊
Zinnia elegans 'Dreamland Scarlet' *p.14*, *Zinnia haageana* 'Persian Carpet' *p.8*

ZINNIA ELEGANS 'ENVY'

INDEX

ACKNOWLEDGMENTS

Picture research Anna Grapes
Picture librarian Neale Chamberlain

Planting plan illustrations Gill Tomblin
Additional illustrations Karen Cochrane
Index Hilary Bird

Dorling Kindersley would like to thank: all staff at
the RHS, in particular Susanne Mitchell, Karen
Wilson and Barbara Haynes at Vincent Square;
Candida Frith-Macdonald for editorial assistance.

American Horticultural Society
Visit AHS at www.ahs.org or call them at
1-800-777-7931 ext. 10. Membership benefits

include *The American Gardener* magazine, free
admission to flower shows, free seed exchange, book
services, and Gardener's Information Service.

Photography
The publisher would like to thank the following for
their kind permission to reproduce their photographs
(key: t=top, b=bottom, r=right, c=center):

John Glover: back cover tl and b, 6, 8tl, 9t, 10br,
11t, 11b, 12b, 13t, 13b, 16b, 17tr, 18, 19b, 21t,
23tl, 25b, 25tl, 35, 38, 39; **Christopher Grey-Wilson:**
5br, 15tl, 25tr, 26bl, 27t; **Photos Horticultural:** front
cover r, back cover tr, 4bl, 9b, 15bl, 23tr, 28, 29, 34;
Daan Smit: 2, 10bl, 14br, 14bc, 15r, 19t, 27b.